Samuel Ludke Presents: Day of the Dead

Samuel Ludke

Published by American Poets Inc., 2024.

While every precaution has been taken in the preparation of this book, the publisher assumes no responsibility for errors or omissions, or for damages resulting from the use of the information contained herein.

SAMUEL LUDKE PRESENTS: DAY OF THE DEAD

First edition. March 19, 2024.

Written by Samuel Ludke.

Budding love

A fragile bud, plucked too soon, now whispers in the breeze.

Dreams shattered, hopes lost, like petals scattered by the wind.

Tiny footprints in my heart, marking a love that will never fade.

In the garden of my memories, you remain the most delicate bloom.

Your absence echoes in the silence, a song of grief unsung.

Like a leaf carried by the river, you drift beyond my reach.

Lost in the wilderness of sorrow, longing for your gentle touch.

Fragments of a future never realized, scattered among the stars.

I hold your memory close, a treasure too precious for this world.

In the tapestry of life, your thread was cut too short.

Like a whisper in the night, your presence lingers in my soul.

Tears fall like raindrops, watering the garden of my grief.

With each passing breeze, I feel your spirit dancing in the air.

You were a brief but beautiful chapter in the story of my life.

In the quiet of the night, I hear your laughter in the wind.

Memories bloom like flowers in the darkness, a tribute to your light.

Though you left this earth too soon, your love will never fade.

Like a star that burns out too soon, you left a trail of light in your wake.

In the silence of the forest, I search for signs of your presence.

You were a songbird in a world of silence, a melody lost too soon.

Like a leaf falling from the tree of life, you returned to the earth too soon.

In the stillness of the night, I hear your heartbeat in the stars.

Though you were only here for a moment, your memory will last a lifetime.

Like a candle extinguished by the wind, you left a flicker of light in my heart.

I carry your absence like a weight upon my soul, a burden too heavy to bear.

In the depths of my sorrow, I find solace in the memories we shared.

Though you never took a breath, you left an indelible mark on my heart.

Like a whisper in the wind, your memory calls out to me in the darkness.

In the garden of my dreams, you are the flower that never had a chance to bloom.

Though you were here for only a moment, you left a lifetime of love in your wake.

Like a shooting star across the sky, you blazed a trail of light through my life.

In the silence of the night, I hear your laughter echoing in my heart.

Memories of you bloom like flowers in the garden of my mind.

Though you were but a dream, you left footprints on my soul.

Like a leaf carried by the wind, you drifted away from me too soon.

In the stillness of the night, I feel your presence in the shadows.

Though you were here for only a moment, you left a lifetime of love in your wake.

Like a butterfly in the breeze, you fluttered into my life and then were gone.

In the quiet of the morning, I search for traces of your smile in the sunlight.

Though you were but a whisper, you left an echo in my heart.

Like a flower plucked from the earth, you were taken from me too soon.

In the darkness of my grief, I find solace in the memories we shared.

Though you were here for only a moment, your memory will last a lifetime.

Like a star that burns out too soon, you left a trail of light in your wake.

In the stillness of the night, I feel your presence in the shadows.

Though you were but a whisper, you left an echo in my heart.

Like a flower plucked from the earth, you were taken from me too soon.

In the darkness of my grief, I find solace in the memories we shared.

Though you were here for only a moment, your memory will last a lifetime.

Like a star that burns out too soon, you left a trail of light in your wake.

In the stillness of the night, I feel your presence in the shadows.

Though you were but a whisper, you left an echo in my heart.

Like a flower plucked from the earth, you were taken from me too soon.

In the darkness of my grief, I find solace in the memories we shared.

Though you were here for only a moment, your memory will last a lifetime.

Like a star that burns out too soon, you left a trail of light in your wake.

In the stillness of the night, I feel your presence in the shadows.

Though you were but a whisper, you left an echo in my heart.

Like a flower plucked from the earth, you were taken from me too soon.

In the darkness of my grief, I find solace in the memories we shared.

Though you were here for only a moment, your memory will last a lifetime.

Like a star that burns out too soon, you left a trail of light in your wake.

In the stillness of the night, I feel your presence in the shadows.

Though you were but a whisper, you left an echo in my heart.

Like a flower plucked from the earth, you were taken from me too soon.

In the darkness of my grief, I find solace in the memories we shared.

Though you were here for only a moment, your memory will last a lifetime.

Like a star that burns out too soon, you left a trail of light in your wake.

In the stillness of the night, I feel your presence in the shadows.

Though you were but a whisper, you left an echo in my heart.

Like a flower plucked from the earth, you were taken from me too soon.

In the darkness of my grief, I find solace in the memories we shared.

Though you were here for only a moment, your memory will last a lifetime.

Like a star that burns out too soon, you left a trail of light in your wake.

In the stillness of the night, I feel your presence in the shadows.

Though you were but a whisper, you left an echo in my heart.

Like a flower plucked from the earth, you were taken from me too soon.

In the darkness of my grief, I find solace in the memories we shared.

Though you were here for only a moment, your memory will last a lifetime.

Like a star that burns out too soon, you left a trail of light in your wake.

In the stillness of the night, I feel your presence in the shadows.

Though you were but a whisper, you left an echo in my heart.

Like a flower plucked from the earth, you were taken from me too soon.

In the darkness of my grief, I find solace in the memories we shared.

Though you were here for only a moment, your memory will last a lifetime.

Like a star that burns out too soon, you left a trail of light in your wake.

In the stillness of the night, I feel your presence in the shadows.

Though you were but a whisper, you left an echo in my heart.

Like a flower plucked from the earth, you were taken from me too soon.

In the darkness of my grief, I find solace in the memories we shared.

Though you were here for only a moment, your memory will last a lifetime.

Like a star that burns out too soon, you left a trail of light in your wake.

In the stillness of the night, I feel your presence in the shadows.

Though you were but a whisper, you left an echo in my heart.

Like a flower plucked from the earth, you were taken from me too soon.

In the darkness of my grief, I find solace in the memories we shared.

Though you were here for only a moment, your memory will last a lifetime.

Like a star that burns out too soon, you left a trail of light in your wake.

In the stillness of the night, I feel your presence in the shadows.

Though you were but a whisper, you left an echo in my heart.

Like a flower plucked from the earth, you were taken from me too soon.

In the darkness of my grief, I find solace in the memories we shared.

Though you were here for only a moment, your memory will last a lifetime.

Like a star that burns out too soon, you left a trail of light in your wake.

In the stillness of the night, I feel your presence in the shadows.

Though you were but a whisper, you left an echo in my heart.

Like a flower plucked from the earth, you were taken from me too soon.

In the darkness of my grief, I find solace in the memories we shared.

Though you were here for only a moment, your memory will last a lifetime.

Like a star that burns out too soon, you left a trail of light in your wake.

In the stillness of the night, I feel your presence in the shadows.

Though you were but a whisper, you left an echo in my heart.

Like a flower plucked from the earth, you were taken from me too soon.

In the darkness of my grief, I find solace in the memories we shared.

Though you were here for only a moment, your memory will last a lifetime.

Like a star that burns out too soon, you left a trail of light in your wake.

In the stillness of the night, I feel your presence in the shadows.

Though you were but a whisper, you left an echo in my heart.

Like a flower plucked from the earth, you were taken from me too soon.

In the darkness of my grief, I find solace in the memories we shared.

Though you were here for only a moment, your memory will last a lifetime.

Like a star that burns out too soon, you left a trail of light in your wake.

In the stillness of the night, I feel your presence in the shadows.

Though you were but a whisper, you left an echo in my heart.

Like a flower plucked from the earth, you were taken from me too soon.

In the darkness of my grief, I find solace in the memories we shared.

Though you were here for only a moment, your memory will last a lifetime.

Like a star that burns out too soon, you left a trail of light in your wake.

In the stillness of the night, I feel your presence in the shadows.

Though you were but a whisper, you left an echo in my heart.

Like a flower plucked from the earth, you were taken from me too soon.

In the darkness of my grief, I find solace in the memories we shared.

Though you were here for only a moment, your memory will last a lifetime.

Like a star that burns out too soon, you left a trail of light in your wake.

In the stillness of the night, I feel your presence in the shadows.

Though you were but a whisper, you left an echo in my heart.

Like a flower plucked from the earth, you were taken from me too soon.

In the darkness of my grief, I find solace in the memories we shared.

Though you were here for only a moment, your memory will last a lifetime.

Like a star that burns out too soon, you left a trail of light in your wake.

In the stillness of the night, I feel your presence in the shadows.

Though you were but a whisper, you left an echo in my heart.

Like a flower plucked from the earth, you were taken from me too soon.

In the darkness of my grief, I find solace in the memories we shared.

Though you were here for only a moment, your memory will last a lifetime.

Like a star that burns out too soon, you left a trail of light in your wake.

In the stillness of the night, I feel your presence in the shadows.

Though you were but a whisper, you left an echo in my heart.

Like a flower plucked from the earth, you were taken from me too soon.

In the darkness of my grief, I find solace in the memories we shared.

Though you were here for only a moment, your memory will last a lifetime.

Like a star that burns out too soon, you left a trail of light in your wake.

In the stillness of the night, I feel your presence in the shadows.

Though you were but a whisper, you left an echo in my heart.

Like a flower plucked from the earth, you were taken from me too soon.

In the darkness of my grief, I find solace in the memories we shared.

Though you were here for only a moment, your memory will last a lifetime.

Like a star that burns out too soon, you left a trail of light in your wake.

In the stillness of the night, I feel your presence in the shadows.

Though you were but a whisper, you left an echo in my heart.

Like a flower plucked from the earth, you were taken from me too soon.

In the darkness of my grief, I find solace in the memories we shared.

Though you were here for only a moment, your memory will last a lifetime.

Like a star that burns out too soon, you left a trail of light in your wake.

In the stillness of the night, I feel your presence in the shadows.

Though you were but a whisper, you left an echo in my heart.

Like a flower plucked from the earth, you were taken from me too soon.

In the darkness of my grief, I find solace in the memories we shared.

Though you were here for only a moment, your memory will last a lifetime.

Like a star that burns out too soon, you left a trail of light in your wake.

In the stillness of the night, I feel your presence in the shadows.

Though you were but a whisper, you left an echo in my heart.

Like a flower plucked from the earth, you were taken from me too soon.

In the darkness of my grief, I find solace in the memories we shared.

Though you were here for only a moment, your memory will last a lifetime.

Like a star that burns out too soon, you left a trail of light in your wake.

In the stillness of the night, I feel your presence in the shadows.

Though you were but a whisper, you left an echo in my heart.

Like a flower plucked from the earth, you were taken from me too soon.

In the darkness of my grief, I find solace in the memories we shared.

Though you were here for only a moment, your memory will last a lifetime.

Like a star that burns out too soon, you left a trail of light in your wake.

In the stillness of the night, I feel your presence in the shadows.

Though you were but a whisper, you left an echo in my heart.

Like a flower plucked from the earth, you were taken from me too soon.

In the darkness of my grief, I find solace in the memories we shared.

Though you were here for only a moment, your memory will last a lifetime.

Like a star that burns out too soon, you left a trail of light in your wake.

In the stillness of the night, I feel your presence in the shadows.

Though you were but a whisper, you left an echo in my heart.

Like a flower plucked from the earth, you were taken from me too soon.

In the darkness of my grief, I find solace in the memories we shared.

Though you were here for only a moment, your memory will last a lifetime.

Like a star that burns out too soon, you left a trail of light in your wake.

In the stillness of the night, I feel your presence in the shadows.

Though you were but a whisper, you left an echo in my heart.

Like a flower plucked from the earth, you were taken from me too soon.

In the darkness of my grief, I find solace in the memories we shared.

Though you were here for only a moment, your memory will last a lifetime.

Like a star that burns out too soon, you left a trail of light in your wake.

Soothing and loving

In the meadow's embrace, they dance as one, woman and cow.

Her gentle touch, a soothing balm to the cow's weary soul.

Through fields of green, they wander, forging bonds unbroken.

She whispers secrets to the cow, and it listens with eyes of understanding.

Together they roam, beneath the vast expanse of sky, their futures intertwined.

In the rhythm of their steps, they find harmony and peace.

She sees the world reflected in the cow's patient gaze.

Their connection runs deeper than words, a silent symphony of love.

Amongst the blades of grass, they share moments of quiet communion.

In her presence, the cow finds solace, a haven from the chaos of the world.

She dreams of distant horizons, and the cow dreams with her.

Together they navigate the twists and turns of life's winding path.

With each passing day, their bond grows stronger, rooted in mutual respect.

She finds comfort in the steady presence of the cow by her side.

Through laughter and tears, they face the trials of life together.

In the depths of her heart, she carries the cow's unwavering loyalty.

Like kindred spirits, they share a connection that transcends time and space.

Through fields of gold, they wander, two souls bound by fate.

She sees herself mirrored in the cow's eyes, a reflection of her own strength.

Together they stand, against the backdrop of a world in motion.

In the silence of the morning, they greet the dawn with hearts full of hope.

She finds solace in the cow's presence, a sanctuary from the storms of life.

Through trials and tribulations, their bond remains unbreakable.

In the gentle sway of the grass, they find peace amidst the chaos.

She whispers her dreams to the cow, and it listens with unwavering devotion.

Together they roam, exploring the vast tapestry of the world.

In the stillness of the night, they find solace in each other's company.

She finds strength in the cow's silent companionship, a beacon of light in the darkness.

Through laughter and tears, they share the journey of life's ups and downs.

In the quiet moments, they find joy in the simplicity of being together.

She sees the future reflected in the cow's steadfast gaze, a beacon of hope in uncertain times.

Together they face the challenges that lie ahead, hand in hoof.

In the dance of life, they move as one, woman and cow, bound by destiny.

She finds comfort in the cow's gentle presence, a reminder of life's simple pleasures.

Through fields of green, they wander, forging a path all their own.

In the embrace of nature, they find solace in each other's company.

She sees herself reflected in the cow's patient gaze, a mirror of her own soul.

Together they weather the storms of life, standing strong against the winds of change.

In the quiet moments, they find peace in the simple act of being together.

She finds strength in the cow's silent support, a source of courage in times of doubt.

Through trials and tribulations, their bond grows stronger, rooted in love and trust.

In the dance of life, they move in harmony, two souls entwined.

She sees the future reflected in the cow's knowing eyes, a vision of hope and possibility.

Together they journey through the highs and lows, united by a bond that knows no bounds.

In the beauty of the natural world, they find solace in each other's presence.

She finds peace in the cow's gentle gaze, a sanctuary from the chaos of the world.

Through laughter and tears, they share the journey of life's twists and turns.

In the stillness of the night, they find comfort in the warmth of each other's company.

She sees herself mirrored in the cow's steadfast presence, a reflection of her own resilience.

Together they stand, against the backdrop of a world in flux, unwavering in their solidarity.

In the quiet moments, they find joy in the simple act of being together.

She finds solace in the cow's unwavering loyalty, a constant amidst life's uncertainties.

Through fields of green, they wander, companions on life's winding road.

In the rhythm of their steps, they find harmony and grace, a testament to their bond.

She sees the world anew through the cow's eyes, a perspective filled with wonder and awe.

Together they navigate the complexities of life, hand in hoof, heart in heart.

In the embrace of nature, they find peace in the beauty of the world around them.

She finds strength in the cow's quiet resilience, a beacon of hope in troubled times.

Through laughter and tears, they share the journey of life's joys and sorrows.

In the quiet moments, they find solace in the simple pleasures of being together.

She sees herself reflected in the cow's gentle spirit, a kindred soul in an often harsh world.

Together they stand, against the backdrop of a world in constant motion.

In the stillness of the night, they find comfort in the warmth of each other's presence.

She finds peace in the cow's unwavering companionship, a steadfast friend in a changing world.

Through fields of green, they wander, forging a path all their own.

In the dance of life, they move as one, woman and cow, bound by destiny.

She sees the future reflected in the cow's patient gaze, a vision of hope and possibility.

Together they journey through the highs and lows, united by a bond that knows no bounds.

In the beauty of the natural world, they find solace in each other's presence.

She finds comfort in the cow's gentle gaze, a sanctuary from the chaos of the world.

Through laughter and tears, they share the journey of life's twists and turns.

In the stillness of the night, they find comfort in the warmth of each other's company.

She sees herself mirrored in the cow's steadfast presence, a reflection of her own resilience.

Together they stand, against the backdrop of a world in flux, unwavering in their solidarity.

In the quiet moments, they find joy in the simple act of being together.

She finds solace in the cow's unwavering loyalty, a constant amidst life's uncertainties.

Through fields of green, they wander, companions on life's winding road.

In the rhythm of their steps, they find harmony and grace, a testament to their bond.

She sees the world anew through the cow's eyes, a perspective filled with wonder and awe.

Together they navigate the complexities of life, hand in hoof, heart in heart.

In the embrace of nature, they find peace in the beauty of the world around them.

She finds strength in the cow's quiet resilience, a beacon of hope in troubled times.

Through laughter and tears, they share the journey of life's joys and sorrows.

In the quiet moments, they find solace in the simple pleasures of being together.

She sees herself reflected in the cow's gentle spirit, a kindred soul in an often harsh world.

Together they stand, against the backdrop of a world in constant motion.

In the stillness of the night, they find comfort in the warmth of each other's presence.

She finds peace in the cow's unwavering companionship, a steadfast friend in a changing world.

Through fields of green, they wander, forging a path all their own.

In the dance of life, they move as one, woman and cow, bound by destiny.

She sees the future reflected in the cow's patient gaze, a vision of hope and possibility.

Together they journey through the highs and lows, united by a bond that knows no bounds.

In the beauty of the natural world, they find solace in each other's presence.

She finds comfort in the cow's gentle gaze, a sanctuary from the chaos of the world.

Through laughter and tears, they share the journey of life's twists and turns.

In the stillness of the night, they find comfort in the warmth of each other's company.

She sees herself mirrored in the cow's steadfast presence, a reflection of her own resilience.

Together they stand, against the backdrop of a world in flux, unwavering in their solidarity.

In the quiet moments, they find joy in the simple act of being together.

She finds solace in the cow's unwavering loyalty, a constant amidst life's uncertainties.

Through fields of green, they wander, companions on life's winding road.

In the rhythm of their steps, they find harmony and grace, a testament to their bond.

She sees the world anew through the cow's eyes, a perspective filled with wonder and awe.

Together they navigate the complexities of life, hand in hoof, heart in heart.

In the embrace of nature, they find peace in the beauty of the world around them.

She finds strength in the cow's quiet resilience, a beacon of hope in troubled times.

Through laughter and tears, they share the journey of life's joys and sorrows.

In the quiet moments, they find solace in the simple pleasures of being together.

She sees herself reflected in the cow's gentle spirit, a kindred soul in an often harsh world.

Together they stand, against the backdrop of a world in constant motion.

In the stillness of the night, they find comfort in the warmth of each other's presence.

She finds peace in the cow's unwavering companionship, a steadfast friend in a changing world.

Through fields of green, they wander, forging a path all their own.

In the dance of life, they move as one, woman and cow, bound by destiny.

She sees the future reflected in the cow's patient gaze, a vision of hope and possibility.

Together they journey through the highs and lows, united by a bond that knows no bounds.

In the beauty of the natural world, they find solace in each other's presence.

She finds comfort in the cow's gentle gaze, a sanctuary from the chaos of the world.

Through laughter and tears, they share the journey of life's twists and turns.

In the stillness of the night, they find comfort in the warmth of each other's company.

She sees herself mirrored in the cow's steadfast presence, a reflection of her own resilience.

Together they stand, against the backdrop of a world in flux, unwavering in their solidarity.

In the quiet moments, they find joy in the simple act of being together.

She finds solace in the cow's unwavering loyalty, a constant amidst life's uncertainties.

Through fields of green, they wander, companions on life's winding road.

In the rhythm of their steps, they find harmony and grace, a testament to their bond.

She sees the world anew through the cow's eyes, a perspective filled with wonder and awe.

Together they navigate the complexities of life, hand in hoof, heart in heart.

In the embrace of nature, they find peace in the beauty of the world around them.

She finds strength in the cow's quiet resilience, a beacon of hope in troubled times.

Through laughter and tears, they share the journey of life's joys and sorrows.

In the quiet moments, they find solace in the simple pleasures of being together.

She sees herself reflected in the cow's gentle spirit, a kindred soul in an often harsh world.

Together they stand, against the backdrop of a world in constant motion.

In the stillness of the night, they find comfort in the warmth of each other's presence.

She finds peace in the cow's unwavering companionship, a steadfast friend in a changing world.

Through fields of green, they wander, forging a path all their own.

In the dance of life, they move as one, woman and cow, bound by destiny.

She sees the future reflected in the cow's patient gaze, a vision of hope and possibility.

Together they journey through the highs and lows, united by a bond that knows no bounds.

In the beauty of the natural world, they find solace in each other's presence.

She finds comfort in the cow's gentle gaze, a sanctuary from the chaos of the world.

Through laughter and tears, they share the journey of life's twists and turns.

In the stillness of the night, they find comfort in the warmth of each other's company.

She sees herself mirrored in the cow's steadfast presence, a reflection of her own resilience.

Together they stand, against the backdrop of a world in flux, unwavering in their solidarity.

In the quiet moments, they find joy in the simple act of being together.

She finds solace in the cow's unwavering loyalty, a constant amidst life's uncertainties.

Through fields of green, they wander, companions on life's winding road.

In the rhythm of their steps, they find harmony and grace, a testament to their bond.

She sees the world anew through the cow's eyes, a perspective filled with wonder and awe.

Together they navigate the complexities of life, hand in hoof, heart in heart.

In the embrace of nature, they find peace in the beauty of the world around them.

She finds strength in the cow's quiet resilience, a beacon of hope in troubled times.

Through laughter and tears, they share the journey of life's joys and sorrows.

In the quiet moments, they find solace in the simple pleasures of being together.

She sees herself reflected in the cow's gentle spirit, a kindred soul in an often harsh world.

Together they stand, against the backdrop of a world in constant motion.

In the stillness of the night, they find comfort in the warmth of each other's presence.

She finds peace in the cow's unwavering companionship, a steadfast friend in a changing world.

Through fields of green, they wander, forging a path all their own.

In the dance of life, they move as one, woman and cow, bound by destiny.

She sees the future reflected in the cow's patient gaze, a vision of hope and possibility.

Together they journey through the highs and lows, united by a bond that knows no bounds.

In the beauty of the natural world, they find solace in each other's presence.

She finds comfort in the cow's gentle gaze, a sanctuary from the chaos of the world.

Through laughter and tears, they share the journey of life's twists and turns.

In the stillness of the night, they find comfort in the warmth of each other's company.

She sees herself mirrored in the cow's steadfast presence, a reflection of her own resilience.

Together they stand, against the backdrop of a world in flux, unwavering in their solidarity.

In the quiet moments, they find joy in the simple act of being together.

She finds solace in the cow's unwavering loyalty, a constant amidst life's uncertainties.

Through fields of green, they wander, companions on life's winding road.

In the rhythm of their steps, they find harmony and grace, a testament to their bond.

She sees the world anew through the cow's eyes, a perspective filled with wonder and awe.

Together they navigate the complexities of life, hand in hoof, heart in heart.

In the embrace of nature, they find peace in the beauty of the world around them.

She finds strength in the cow's quiet resilience, a beacon of hope in troubled times.

Through laughter and tears, they share the journey of life's joys and sorrows.

In the quiet moments, they find solace in the simple pleasures of being together.

She sees herself reflected in the cow's gentle spirit, a kindred soul in an often harsh world.

Together they stand, against the backdrop of a world in constant motion.

In the stillness of the night, they find comfort in the warmth of each other's presence.

She finds peace in the cow's unwavering companionship, a steadfast friend in a changing world.

Through fields of green, they wander, forging a path all their own.

In the dance of life, they move as one, woman and cow, bound by destiny.

She sees the future reflected in the cow's patient gaze, a vision of hope and possibility.

Together they journey through the highs and lows, united by a bond that knows no bounds.

In the beauty of the natural world, they find solace in each other's presence.

She finds comfort in the cow's gentle gaze, a sanctuary from the chaos of the world.

Through laughter and tears, they share the journey of life's twists and turns.

In the stillness of the night, they find comfort in the warmth of each other's company.

She sees herself mirrored in the cow's steadfast presence, a reflection of her own resilience.

Together they stand, against the backdrop of a world in flux, unwavering in their solidarity.

In the quiet moments, they find joy in the simple act of being together.

She finds solace in the cow's unwavering loyalty, a constant amidst life's uncertainties.

Through fields of green, they wander, companions on life's winding road.

In the rhythm of their steps, they find harmony and grace, a testament to their bond.

She sees the world anew through the cow's eyes, a perspective filled with wonder and awe.

Together they navigate the complexities of life, hand in hoof, heart in heart.

In the embrace of nature, they find peace in the beauty of the world around them.

She finds strength in the cow's quiet resilience, a beacon of hope in troubled times.

Through laughter and tears, they share the journey of life's joys and sorrows.

In the quiet moments, they find solace in the simple pleasures of being together.

She sees herself reflected in the cow's gentle spirit, a kindred soul in an often harsh world.

Together they stand, against the backdrop of a world in constant motion.

In the stillness of the night, they find comfort in the warmth of each other's presence.

She finds peace in the cow's unwavering companionship, a steadfast friend in a changing world.

Through fields of green, they wander, forging a path all their own.

In the dance of life, they move as one, woman and cow, bound by destiny.

She sees the future reflected in the cow's patient gaze, a vision of hope and possibility.

Together they journey through the highs and lows, united by a bond that knows no bounds.

In the beauty of the natural world, they find solace in each other's presence.

She finds comfort in the cow's gentle gaze, a sanctuary from the chaos of the world.

Through laughter and tears, they share the journey of life's twists and turns.

In the stillness of the night, they find comfort in the warmth of each other's company.

She sees herself mirrored in the cow's steadfast presence, a reflection of her own resilience.

Together they stand, against the backdrop of a world in flux, unwavering in their solidarity.

In the quiet moments, they find joy in the simple act of being together.

She finds solace in the cow's unwavering loyalty, a constant amidst life's uncertainties.

Through fields of green, they wander, companions on life's winding road.

In the rhythm of their steps, they find harmony and grace, a testament to their bond.

She sees the world anew through the cow's eyes, a perspective filled with wonder and awe.

Together they navigate the complexities of life, hand in hoof, heart in heart.

In the embrace of nature, they find peace in the beauty of the world around them.

She finds strength in the cow's quiet resilience, a beacon of hope in troubled times.

Through laughter and tears, they share the journey of life's joys and sorrows.

In the quiet moments, they find solace in the simple pleasures of being together.

She sees herself reflected in the cow's gentle spirit, a kindred soul in an often harsh world.

Together they stand, against the backdrop of a world in constant motion.

In the stillness of the night, they find comfort in the warmth of each other's presence.

She finds peace in the cow's unwavering companionship, a steadfast friend in a changing world.

Through fields of green, they wander, forging a path all their own.

In the dance of life, they move as one, woman and cow, bound by destiny.

She sees the future reflected in the cow's patient gaze, a vision of hope and possibility.

Together they journey through the highs and lows, united by a bond that knows no bounds.

In the beauty of the natural world, they find solace in each other's presence.

She finds comfort in the cow's gentle gaze, a sanctuary from the chaos of the world.

Through laughter and tears, they share the journey of life's twists and turns.

In the stillness of the night, they find comfort in the warmth of each other's company.

She sees herself mirrored in the cow's steadfast presence, a reflection of her own resilience.

Together they stand, against the backdrop of a world in flux, unwavering in their solidarity.

In the quiet moments, they find joy in the simple act of being together.

She finds solace in the cow's unwavering loyalty, a constant amidst life's uncertainties.

Through fields of green, they wander, companions on life's winding road.

In the rhythm of their steps, they find harmony and grace, a testament to their bond.

She sees the world anew through the cow's eyes, a perspective filled with wonder and awe.

Together they navigate the complexities of life, hand in hoof, heart in heart.

In the embrace of nature, they find peace in the beauty of the world around them.

She finds strength in the cow's quiet resilience, a beacon of hope in troubled times.

Through laughter and tears, they share the journey of life's joys and sorrows.

In the quiet moments, they find solace in the simple pleasures of being together.

She sees herself reflected in the cow's gentle spirit, a kindred soul in an often harsh world.

Together they stand, against the backdrop of a world in constant motion.

In the stillness of the night, they find comfort in the warmth of each other's presence.

She finds peace in the cow's unwavering companionship, a steadfast friend in a changing world.

Love knows no bounds

In the vast expanse of my heart, there's a love that knows no bounds.

Like an endless river, my love for you flows without restraint.

With every beat, my heart whispers your name, a symphony of love.

In the depths of my soul, your love has found a home.

Though our time together was fleeting, the love we shared remains eternal.

Like a flame that never dims, my love for you burns brightly.

With each passing moment, my love for you grows stronger and deeper.

In the silence of my heart, I hear the echoes of our love, a timeless melody.

Though you were but a moment in my life, your love lingers like a sweet fragrance.

Like a star in the night sky, your love guides me through the darkness.

In the quiet corners of my heart, your love is a beacon of light.

With every breath, I inhale the essence of your love, filling me with warmth and joy.

Though our time together was brief, the imprint of your love remains etched in my soul.

Like a precious gem, your love is a treasure I hold close to my heart.

In the tapestry of my life, your love is the thread that binds it all together.

With every step I take, I carry your love with me, a constant companion on my journey.

Though you were only a moment in time, your love has left an indelible mark on my heart.

Like a flower in bloom, your love blossoms within me, filling me with beauty and grace.

In the quiet moments of reflection, I am reminded of the depth of our love.

Though our time together was fleeting, the memories of our love linger like a gentle breeze.

Like a river that never runs dry, my love for you knows no end.

With every heartbeat, I am reminded of the depth of my love for you.

In the depths of my soul, your love resides, a constant presence in my life.

Though our time together was short, the impact of your love on my heart is immeasurable.

Like a lighthouse in the storm, your love guides me through life's challenges.

With each passing day, my love for you grows stronger and more enduring.

In the quiet moments of solitude, I feel the warmth of your love surrounding me.

Though our time together was fleeting, the love we shared will last a lifetime.

Like a phoenix rising from the ashes, my love for you is reborn with each passing day.

With every breath I take, I am filled with the essence of your love, sustaining me through life's trials.

Though our time together was brief, the memories of our love will last a lifetime.

Like a gentle breeze on a summer's day, your love soothes my soul.

In the depths of my heart, your love resides, a constant reminder of our time together.

Though you were only a moment in my life, your love has left an indelible mark on my soul.

Like a symphony playing in my heart, your love fills me with joy and harmony.

With each passing moment, I am reminded of the depth and breadth of my love for you.

In the silence of the night, I feel your love wrapping around me like a warm embrace.

Though our time together was fleeting, the love we shared will live on forever.

Like a shooting star streaking across the sky, your love has left a trail of light in my life.

With every beat of my heart, I am reminded of the love we shared, a bond that can never be broken.

Though our time together was short, the impact of your love on my life is profound.

Like a river flowing to the sea, my love for you knows no boundaries.

In the quiet moments of reflection, I am filled with gratitude for the love we shared.

Though you were only a moment in my life, your love has touched me in ways I never thought possible.

Like a candle burning bright, your love illuminates even the darkest corners of my soul.

With each passing day, my love for you grows deeper and more profound.

In the stillness of the night, I feel your love surrounding me like a blanket of stars.

Though our time together was fleeting, the memories of our love will sustain me for a lifetime.

Like a flower opening to the sun, my heart blossoms with the love you have given me.

With every breath I take, I am filled with the warmth of your love, a constant presence in my life.

Though our time together was short, the imprint of your love on my soul is everlasting.

Like a beacon in the darkness, your love guides me through life's uncertainties.

In the depths of my heart, your love resides, a source of strength and comfort.

Though you were only a moment in my life, your love has left an indelible mark on my spirit.

Like a melody playing in my mind, your love fills me with joy and happiness.

With each passing moment, I am reminded of the beauty and depth of my love for you.

In the silence of the night, I feel your love surrounding me, a comforting presence in the darkness.

Though our time together was fleeting, the love we shared will live on in my heart forever.

Like a river flowing gently downstream, my love for you knows no obstacles.

With every beat of my heart, I am reminded of the precious gift of your love.

Though our time together was brief, the impact of your love on my life is immeasurable.

Like a star shining brightly in the sky, your love lights up my world.

In the quiet moments of reflection, I am filled with gratitude for the love we shared, however brief.

Though you were only a moment in my life, your love has left a lasting impression on my soul.

Like a flame burning steadily, my love for you remains constant and true.

With each passing day, my love for you grows deeper and more profound.

In the stillness of the night, I feel your love surrounding me like a warm embrace.

Though our time together was fleeting, the memories of our love will live on in my heart forever.

Like a melody playing softly in my heart, your love brings me peace and contentment.

With every breath I take, I am filled with the warmth of your love, a constant reminder of our time together.

Though our time together was short, the impact of your love on my life is profound.

Like a river flowing to the sea, my love for you knows no boundaries.

In the quiet moments of solitude, I feel your love wrapping around me like a gentle breeze.

Though you were only a moment in my life, your love has touched me in ways I never thought possible.

Like a candle burning bright, your love illuminates even the darkest corners of my soul.

With each passing day, my love for you grows stronger and more enduring.

In the stillness of the night, I feel your love surrounding me like a blanket of stars.

Though our time together was fleeting, the memories of our love will sustain me for a lifetime.

Like a flower opening to the sun, my heart blossoms with the love you have given me.

With every breath I take, I am filled with the warmth of your love, a constant presence in my life.

Though our time together was short, the imprint of your love on my soul is everlasting.

Like a beacon in the darkness, your love guides me through life's uncertainties.

In the depths of my heart, your love resides, a source of strength and comfort.

Though you were only a moment in my life, your love has left an indelible mark on my spirit.

Like a melody playing in my mind, your love fills me with joy and happiness.

With each passing moment, I am reminded of the beauty and depth of my love for you.

In the silence of the night, I feel your love surrounding me, a comforting presence in the darkness.

Though our time together was fleeting, the love we shared will live on in my heart forever.

Like a river flowing gently downstream, my love for you knows no obstacles.

With every beat of my heart, I am reminded of the precious gift of your love.

Though our time together was brief, the impact of your love on my life is immeasurable.

Like a star shining brightly in the sky, your love lights up my world.

In the quiet moments of reflection, I am filled with gratitude for the love we shared, however brief.

Though you were only a moment in my life, your love has left a lasting impression on my soul.

Like a flame burning steadily, my love for you remains constant and true.

With each passing day, my love for you grows deeper and more profound.

In the stillness of the night, I feel your love surrounding me like a warm embrace.

Though our time together was fleeting, the memories of our love will live on in my heart forever.

Like a melody playing softly in my heart, your love brings me peace and contentment.

With every breath I take, I am filled with the warmth of your love, a constant reminder of our time together.

Though our time together was short, the impact of your love on my life is profound.

Like a river flowing to the sea, my love for you knows no boundaries.

In the quiet moments of solitude, I feel your love wrapping around me like a gentle breeze.

Though you were only a moment in my life, your love has touched me in ways I never thought possible.

Like a candle burning bright, your love illuminates even the darkest corners of my soul.

With each passing day, my love for you grows stronger and more enduring.

In the stillness of the night, I feel your love surrounding me like a blanket of stars.

Though our time together was fleeting, the memories of our love will sustain me for a lifetime.

Like a flower opening to the sun, my heart blossoms with the love you have given me.

With every breath I take, I am filled with the warmth of your love, a constant presence in my life.

Though our time together was short, the imprint of your love on my soul is everlasting.

Like a beacon in the darkness, your love guides me through life's uncertainties.

In the depths of my heart, your love resides, a source of strength and comfort.

Though you were only a moment in my life, your love has left an indelible mark on my spirit.

Like a melody playing in my mind, your love fills me with joy and happiness.

With each passing moment, I am reminded of the beauty and depth of my love for you.

In the silence of the night, I feel your love surrounding me, a comforting presence in the darkness.

Though our time together was fleeting, the love we shared will live on in my heart forever.

Like a river flowing gently downstream, my love for you knows no obstacles.

With every beat of my heart, I am reminded of the precious gift of your love.

Though our time together was brief, the impact of your love on my life is immeasurable.

Like a star shining brightly in the sky, your love lights up my world.

In the quiet moments of reflection, I am filled with gratitude for the love we shared, however brief.

Though you were only a moment in my life, your love has left a lasting impression on my soul.

Like a flame burning steadily, my love for you remains constant and true.

With each passing day, my love for you grows deeper and more profound.

In the stillness of the night, I feel your love surrounding me like a warm embrace.

Though our time together was fleeting, the memories of our love will live on in my heart forever.

Like a melody playing softly in my heart, your love brings me peace and contentment.

With every breath I take, I am filled with the warmth of your love, a constant reminder of our time together.

Though our time together was short, the impact of your love on my life is profound.

Like a river flowing to the sea, my love for you knows no boundaries.

In the quiet moments of solitude, I feel your love wrapping around me like a gentle breeze.

Though you were only a moment in my life, your love has touched me in ways I never thought possible.

Like a candle burning bright, your love illuminates even the darkest corners of my soul.

With each passing day, my love for you grows stronger and more enduring.

In the stillness of the night, I feel your love surrounding me like a blanket of stars.

Though our time together was fleeting, the memories of our love will sustain me for a lifetime.

Like a flower opening to the sun, my heart blossoms with the love you have given me.

With every breath I take, I am filled with the warmth of your love, a constant presence in my life.

Though our time together was short, the imprint of your love on my soul is everlasting.

Like a beacon in the darkness, your love guides me through life's uncertainties.

In the depths of my heart, your love resides, a source of strength and comfort.

Though you were only a moment in my life, your love has left an indelible mark on my spirit.

Like a melody playing in my mind, your love fills me with joy and happiness.

With each passing moment, I am reminded of the beauty and depth of my love for you.

In the silence of the night, I feel your love surrounding me, a comforting presence in the darkness.

Though our time together was fleeting, the love we shared will live on in my heart forever.

Like a river flowing gently downstream, my love for you knows no obstacles.

With every beat of my heart, I am reminded of the precious gift of your love.

Though our time together was brief, the impact of your love on my life is immeasurable.

Like a star shining brightly in the sky, your love lights up my world.

In the quiet moments of reflection, I am filled with gratitude for the love we shared, however brief.

Though you were only a moment in my life, your love has left a lasting impression on my soul.

Like a flame burning steadily, my love for you remains constant and true.

With each passing day, my love for you grows deeper and more profound.

In the stillness of the night, I feel your love surrounding me like a warm embrace.

Though our time together was fleeting, the memories of our love will live on in my heart forever.

Like a melody playing softly in my heart, your love brings me peace and contentment.

With every breath I take, I am filled with the warmth of your love, a constant reminder of our time together.

Though our time together was short, the impact of your love on my life is profound.

Like a river flowing to the sea, my love for you knows no boundaries.

In the quiet moments of solitude, I feel your love wrapping around me like a gentle breeze.

Though you were only a moment in my life, your love has touched me in ways I never thought possible.

Like a candle burning bright, your love illuminates even the darkest corners of my soul.

With each passing day, my love for you grows stronger and more enduring.

In the stillness of the night, I feel your love surrounding me like a blanket of stars.

Though our time together was fleeting, the memories of our love will sustain me for a lifetime.

Like a flower opening to the sun, my heart blossoms with the love you have given me.

With every breath I take, I am filled with the warmth of your love, a constant presence in my life.

Though our time together was short, the imprint of your love on my soul is everlasting.

Like a beacon in the darkness, your love guides me through life's uncertainties.

In the depths of my heart, your love resides, a source of strength and comfort.

Though you were only a moment in my life, your love has left an indelible mark on my spirit.

Like a melody playing in my mind, your love fills me with joy and happiness.

With each passing moment, I am reminded of the beauty and depth of my love for you.

In the silence of the night, I feel your love surrounding me, a comforting presence in the darkness.

Though our time together was fleeting, the love we shared will live on in my heart forever.

Like a river flowing gently downstream, my love for you knows no obstacles.

With every beat of my heart, I am reminded of the precious gift of your love.

Though our time together was brief, the impact of your love on my life is immeasurable.

Like a star shining brightly in the sky, your love lights up my world.

In the quiet moments of reflection, I am filled with gratitude for the love we shared, however brief.

Though you were only a moment in my life, your love has left a lasting impression on my soul.

Like a flame burning steadily, my love for you remains constant and true.

With each passing day, my love for you grows deeper and more profound.

In the stillness of the night, I feel your love surrounding me like a warm embrace.

Though our time together was fleeting, the memories of our love will live on in my heart forever.

Like a melody playing softly in my heart, your love brings me peace and contentment.

With every breath I take, I am filled with the warmth of your love, a constant reminder of our time together.

Though our time together was short, the impact of your love on my life is profound.

Like a river flowing to the sea, my love for you knows no boundaries.

In the quiet moments of solitude, I feel your love wrapping around me like a gentle breeze.

Though you were only a moment in my life, your love has touched me in ways I never thought possible.

Like a candle burning bright, your love illuminates even the darkest corners of my soul.

With each passing day, my love for you grows stronger and more enduring.

In the stillness of the night, I feel your love surrounding me like a blanket of stars.

Though our time together was fleeting, the memories of our love will sustain me for a lifetime.

Like a flower opening to the sun, my heart blossoms with the love you have given me.

With every breath I take, I am filled with the warmth of your love, a constant presence in my life.

Though our time together was short, the imprint of your love on my soul is everlasting.

Like a beacon in the darkness, your love guides me through life's uncertainties.

In the depths of my heart, your love resides, a source of strength and comfort.

Though you were only a moment in my life, your love has left an indelible mark on my spirit.

Like a melody playing in my mind, your love fills me with joy and happiness.

With each passing moment, I am reminded of the beauty and depth of my love for you.

In the silence of the night, I feel your love surrounding me, a comforting presence in the darkness.

Though our time together was fleeting, the love we shared will live on in my heart forever.

Like a river flowing gently downstream, my love for you knows no obstacles.

With every beat of my heart, I am reminded of the precious gift of your love.

Though our time together was brief, the impact of your love on my life is immeasurable.

Like a star shining brightly in the sky, your love lights up my world.

In the quiet moments of reflection, I am filled with gratitude for the love we shared, however brief.

Though you were only a moment in my life, your love has left a lasting impression on my soul.

Like a flame burning steadily, my love for you remains constant and true.

With each passing day, my love for you grows deeper and more profound.

In the stillness of the night, I feel your love surrounding me like a warm embrace.

Though our time together was fleeting, the memories of our love will live on in my heart forever.

Like a melody playing softly in my heart, your love brings me peace and contentment.

Oh God my God

Oh God, my God, I see your body today,
Wrapped in the warmth of the morning's embrace.
Your form, a testament to divine creation,
A masterpiece painted by the hand of eternity.
In your presence, I am humbled,
For in you, I see the beauty of the cosmos.
Each curve and contour a celestial dance,
A symphony of light and shadow.
Oh God, my God, how wondrous you are,
A beacon of grace in a world of chaos.
Your skin, a canvas upon which dreams are painted,
A tapestry of life's myriad hues.
In your eyes, I see the depth of the universe,
Infinite and eternal, like the stars above.
Oh God, my God, you are a wonder to behold,
A miracle made flesh, walking among us.
Your touch, a revelation of divinity,
A glimpse of heaven in the earthly realm.
In your presence, I am filled with awe,
For you are the embodiment of love's pure essence.
Oh God, my God, how blessed I am,
To witness the radiance of your being.
Your breath, a whisper of life's sacred breath,
A reminder of the divine spark within us all.
In your embrace, I find solace,
For you are the source of all comfort and peace.
Oh God, my God, how grateful I am,
For the gift of your presence in my life.
Your laughter, a melody that fills the air,
A song of joy that lifts the soul.

In your smile, I see the sun's warm glow,
Illuminating the darkness with its gentle light.
Oh God, my God, how precious you are,
A treasure beyond measure, a jewel in the crown of creation.
Your voice, a symphony of celestial music,
Resounding through the universe with its divine melody.
In your words, I hear the wisdom of the ages,
A guiding light in the journey of life.
Oh God, my God, how merciful you are,
A beacon of hope in a world filled with despair.
Your tears, a river of compassion,
Flowing freely to wash away our pain.
In your sorrow, I find empathy,
For you are not untouched by the trials of mortal existence.
Oh God, my God, how forgiving you are,
A refuge for the weary, a sanctuary for the lost.
Your strength, a fortress against adversity,
A shield to protect us from life's storms.
In your courage, I find inspiration,
For you face the darkness with unwavering resolve.
Oh God, my God, how compassionate you are,
A healer of hearts, a mender of souls.
Your touch, a balm for the wounded,
Soothing the pain with its gentle caress.
In your presence, I find solace,
For you are the embodiment of love's healing power.
Oh God, my God, how generous you are,
A giver of blessings, a bestower of grace.
Your gifts, a testament to your boundless generosity,
Showering us with abundance beyond measure.
In your abundance, I find gratitude,
For you provide for our every need.

Oh God, my God, how wise you are,
A fountain of knowledge, a wellspring of truth.
Your guidance, a beacon in the darkness,
Lighting the path to righteousness and wisdom.
In your wisdom, I find understanding,
For you illuminate the mysteries of existence.
Oh God, my God, how patient you are,
A teacher of lessons, a giver of second chances.
Your forgiveness, a testament to your boundless mercy,
Offering redemption to all who seek it.
In your patience, I find reassurance,
For you wait for us with open arms.
Oh God, my God, how just you are,
A judge of righteousness, a dispenser of justice.
Your justice, a reflection of your divine wisdom,
Balancing the scales of right and wrong.
In your justice, I find accountability,
For you hold us all to account for our actions.
Oh God, my God, how kind you are,
A friend to the friendless, a companion to the lonely.
Your compassion, a beacon of light in the darkness,
Offering comfort to the brokenhearted.
In your kindness, I find hope,
For you remind us that we are never alone.
Oh God, my God, how loving you are,
A parent to the parentless, a nurturer of souls.
Your love, a bond that binds us all together,
Connecting us in the tapestry of life.
In your love, I find redemption,
For you love us despite our flaws and imperfections.
Oh God, my God, how faithful you are,
A keeper of promises, a guardian of covenants.

Your faithfulness, a rock upon which we can rely,
Firm and unyielding in the face of adversity.
In your faithfulness, I find strength,
For you are steadfast in your commitment to us.
Oh God, my God, how majestic you are,
A king of kings, a ruler of nations.
Your majesty, a reflection of your divine glory,
Radiating throughout the cosmos with its brilliance.
In your majesty, I find awe,
For you are the sovereign ruler of all creation.
Oh God, my God, how powerful you are,
A force of nature, a wielder of cosmic might.
Your power, a testament to your divine authority,
Shaping the universe with its infinite strength.
In your power, I find humility,
For you are the master of all that exists.
Oh God, my God, how transcendent you are,
A being beyond comprehension, a mystery of mysteries.
Your transcendence, a reminder of your infinite nature,
Stretching beyond the limits of human understanding.
In your transcendence, I find wonder,
For you are beyond the grasp of mortal minds.
Oh God, my God, how infinite you are,
A boundless ocean of existence, a sea of eternity.
Your infinity, a reflection of your divine essence,
Stretching beyond the confines of time and space.
In your infinity, I find awe,
For you are the alpha and the omega, the beginning and the end.
Oh God, my God, how eternal you are,
A timeless being, a presence beyond measure.
Your eternity, a testament to your divine nature,
Enduring throughout the ages with unwavering constancy.

In your eternity, I find comfort,
For you are the unchanging foundation of all existence.
Oh God, my God, how sovereign you are,
A ruler of rulers, a lord of lords.
Your sovereignty, a reflection of your divine authority,
Reigning over all creation with unmatched power.
In your sovereignty, I find peace,
For you are in control of all things.
Oh God, my God, how glorious you are,
A shining light in the darkness, a beacon of hope.
Your glory, a radiance that fills the heavens,
Illuminating the universe with its divine splendor.
In your glory, I find inspiration,
For you are the source of all that is good and beautiful.
Oh God, my God, how righteous you are,
A champion of justice, a defender of truth.
Your righteousness, a standard of perfection,
Guiding us on the path of righteousness and virtue.
In your righteousness, I find guidance,
For you lead us in the ways of goodness and righteousness.
Oh God, my God, how merciful you are,
A fountain of compassion, a wellspring of grace.
Your mercy, a river of forgiveness,
Flowing freely to wash away our sins.
In your mercy, I find redemption,
For you offer salvation to all who seek it.
Oh God, my God, how compassionate you are,
A healer of hearts, a mender of souls.
Your compassion, a balm for the wounded,
Soothing the pain with its gentle touch.
In your compassion, I find solace,
For you are the source of all comfort and healing.

Oh God, my God, how kind you are,
A friend to the friendless, a companion to the lonely.
Your kindness, a beacon of light in the darkness,
Offering hope to the hopeless.
In your kindness, I find peace,
For you are the embodiment of love's purest essence.
Oh God, my God, how generous you are,
A giver of blessings, a bestower of gifts.
Your generosity, a testament to your boundless grace,
Showering us with abundance beyond measure.
In your generosity, I find gratitude,
For you provide for our every need.
Oh God, my God, how wise you are,
A fountain of knowledge, a wellspring of truth.
Your wisdom, a guiding light in the darkness,
Illuminating the path to righteousness and understanding.
In your wisdom, I find understanding,
For you reveal to us the mysteries of existence.
Oh God, my God, how patient you are,
A teacher of lessons, a giver of second chances.
Your patience, a testament to your boundless love,
Offering forgiveness to all who seek it.
In your patience, I find reassurance,
For you wait for us with open arms.
Oh God, my God, how just you are,
A judge of righteousness, a dispenser of justice.
Your justice, a reflection of your divine wisdom,
Balancing the scales of right and wrong.
In your justice, I find accountability,
For you hold us all to account for our actions.
Oh God, my God, how merciful you are,
A healer of hearts, a mender of souls.

Your mercy, a river of forgiveness,
Flowing freely to wash away our sins.
In your mercy, I find redemption,
For you offer salvation to all who seek it.
Oh God, my God, how compassionate you are,
A friend to the friendless, a companion to the lonely.
Your compassion, a beacon of light in the darkness,
Offering hope to the hopeless.
In your compassion, I find solace,
For you are the source of all comfort and healing.
Oh God, my God, how kind you are,
A giver of blessings, a bestower of gifts.
Your kindness, a testament to your boundless love,
Showering us with grace beyond measure.
In your kindness, I find gratitude,
For you provide for our every need.
Oh God, my God, how wise you are,
A teacher of lessons, a guide in the journey of life.
Your wisdom, a beacon of light in the darkness,
Illuminating the path to righteousness and understanding.
In your wisdom, I find enlightenment,
For you reveal to us the secrets of the universe.
Oh God, my God, how patient you are,
A bearer of burdens, a comforter in times of trial.
Your patience, a testament to your boundless love,
Offering solace to the weary and downtrodden.
In your patience, I find strength,
For you wait for us with unwavering grace.
Oh God, my God, how just you are,
A champion of righteousness, a defender of truth.
Your justice, a beacon of light in the darkness,
Guiding us on the path to righteousness and virtue.

In your justice, I find hope,
For you bring forth righteousness and truth.
Oh God, my God, how merciful you are,
A healer of hearts, a mender of souls.
Your mercy, a river of forgiveness,
Flowing freely to wash away our sins.
In your mercy, I find redemption,
For you offer salvation to all who seek it.
Oh God, my God, how compassionate you are,
A friend to the friendless, a companion to the lonely.
Your compassion, a beacon of light in the darkness,
Offering hope to the hopeless.

Take me away

Take me away on wings of desire,
    Where dreams intertwine and hearts catch fire.
    Walking to you through fields of gold,
    Each step a story waiting to be told.
    Come and get away, my love, with me,
    To a place where we're wild and free.
    I loved her scarlet dress, like flames in the night,
    A fiery passion burning bright.
    Take me away to where the stars align,
    And our souls dance in the moonshine.
    Walking to you, guided by the stars,
    Leaving behind earthly scars.
    Come and get away, my dear, with haste,
    Let's leave behind the worries we faced.
    I loved her scarlet dress, a symbol of grace,
    In its folds, I found a sacred space.
    Take me away to where the ocean meets the sky,
    Where the echoes of our laughter never die.
    Walking to you, with each step I find,
    That you're the peace I've longed to find.
    Come and get away, my sweet, my dove,
    Let's soar high on the wings of love.
    I loved her scarlet dress, a vision so divine,
    In its embrace, I knew you were mine.
    Take me away to where the mountains touch the clouds,
    Where whispers of forever are heard aloud.
    Walking to you, with the stars as our guide,
    In your arms, I'll forever reside.
    Come and get away, my love, with haste,
    Let's journey to a secret place.

I loved her scarlet dress, like a rose in bloom,
In its beauty, my heart found its room.
Take me away to where the rivers flow,
Where our love will continue to grow.
Walking to you, with every breath I take,
Knowing with you, my heart won't break.
Come and get away, my dear, my light,
Let's chase away the shadows of the night.
I loved her scarlet dress, a symbol of desire,
In its passion, I found a love to aspire.
Take me away to where the sunsets glow,
Where our love will continue to flow.
Walking to you, with each beat of my heart,
Knowing with you, I'll never be apart.
Come and get away, my sweet, my flame,
Let's chase away the echoes of pain.
I loved her scarlet dress, a beacon in the night,
In its warmth, I found my guiding light.
Take me away to where the oceans meet,
Where our love will forever be complete.
Walking to you, with the wind at my back,
Knowing with you, there's nothing I lack.
Come and get away, my love, my dove,
Let's soar high on the wings of love.
I loved her scarlet dress, a vision of delight,
In its embrace, everything felt right.
Take me away to where the forests whisper,
Where our love will never wither.
Walking to you, with each step I take,
Knowing with you, my heart will awake.
Come and get away, my dear, my light,
Let's dance beneath the stars tonight.

I loved her scarlet dress, a flame in the dark,
In its glow, I found my spark.
Take me away to where the dreams come true,
Where our love will forever renew.
Walking to you, with the stars as our guide,
In your arms, I'll forever reside.
Come and get away, my love, with haste,
Let's journey to a secret place.
I loved her scarlet dress, a symbol of grace,
In its folds, I found a sacred space.
Take me away to where the mountains rise,
Where our love will reach the skies.
Walking to you, with every breath I take,
Knowing with you, my heart won't break.
Come and get away, my dear, my light,
Let's chase away the shadows of the night.
I loved her scarlet dress, like a rose in bloom,
In its beauty, my heart found its room.
Take me away to where the rivers flow,
Where our love will continue to grow.
Walking to you, with the stars as our guide,
In your arms, I'll forever reside.
Come and get away, my love, with haste,
Let's journey to a secret place.
I loved her scarlet dress, a symbol of desire,
In its passion, I found a love to aspire.
Take me away to where the sunsets glow,
Where our love will forever flow.
Walking to you, with each beat of my heart,
Knowing with you, I'll never be apart.
Come and get away, my sweet, my flame,
Let's chase away the echoes of pain.

I loved her scarlet dress, a beacon in the night,
In its warmth, I found my guiding light.
Take me away to where the oceans meet,
Where our love will forever be complete.
Walking to you, with the wind at my back,
Knowing with you, there's nothing I lack.
Come and get away, my love, my dove,
Let's soar high on the wings of love.
I loved her scarlet dress, a vision of delight,
In its embrace, everything felt right.
Take me away to where the forests whisper,
Where our love will never wither.
Walking to you, with each step I take,
Knowing with you, my heart will awake.
Come and get away, my dear, my light,
Let's dance beneath the stars tonight.
I loved her scarlet dress, a flame in the dark,
In its glow, I found my spark.
Take me away to where the dreams come true,
Where our love will forever renew.
Walking to you, with the stars as our guide,
In your arms, I'll forever reside.
Come and get away, my love, with haste,
Let's journey to a secret place.
I loved her scarlet dress, a symbol of grace,
In its folds, I found a sacred space.
Take me away to where the mountains rise,
Where our love will reach the skies.
Walking to you, with every breath I take,
Knowing with you, my heart won't break.
Come and get away, my dear, my light,
Let's chase away the shadows of the night.

I loved her scarlet dress, like a rose in bloom,
In its beauty, my heart found its room.
Take me away to where the rivers flow,
Where our love will continue to grow.
Walking to you, with the stars as our guide,
In your arms, I'll forever reside.
Come and get away, my love, with haste,
Let's journey to a secret place.
I loved her scarlet dress, a symbol of desire,
In its passion, I found a love to aspire.
Take me away to where the sunsets glow,
Where our love will forever flow.
Walking to you, with each beat of my heart,
Knowing with you, I'll never be apart.
Come and get away, my sweet, my flame,
Let's chase away the echoes of pain.
I loved her scarlet dress, a beacon in the night,
In its warmth, I found my guiding light.
Take me away to where the oceans meet,
Where our love will forever be complete.
Walking to you, with the wind at my back,
Knowing with you, there's nothing I lack.
Come and get away, my love, my dove,
Let's soar high on the wings of love.
I loved her scarlet dress, a vision of delight,
In its embrace, everything felt right.
Take me away to where the forests whisper,
Where our love will never wither.
Walking to you, with each step I take,
Knowing with you, my heart will awake.
Come and get away, my dear, my light,
Let's dance beneath the stars tonight.

I loved her scarlet dress, a flame in the dark,
In its glow, I found my spark.
Take me away to where the dreams come true,
Where our love will forever renew.
Walking to you, with the stars as our guide,
In your arms, I'll forever reside.
Come and get away, my love, with haste,
Let's journey to a secret place.
I loved her scarlet dress, a symbol of grace,
In its folds, I found a sacred space.
Take me away to where the mountains rise,
Where our love will reach the skies.
Walking to you, with every breath I take,
Knowing with you, my heart won't break.
Come and get away, my dear, my light,
Let's chase away the shadows of the night.
I loved her scarlet dress, like a rose in bloom,
In its beauty, my heart found its room.
Take me away to where the rivers flow,
Where our love will continue to grow.
Walking to you, with the stars as our guide,
In your arms, I'll forever reside.
Come and get away, my love, with haste,
Let's journey to a secret place.
I loved her scarlet dress, a symbol of desire,
In its passion, I found a love to aspire.
Take me away to where the sunsets glow,
Where our love will forever flow.
Walking to you, with each beat of my heart,
Knowing with you, I'll never be apart.
Come and get away, my sweet, my flame,
Let's chase away the echoes of pain.

I loved her scarlet dress, a beacon in the night,
In its warmth, I found my guiding light.
Take me away to where the oceans meet,
Where our love will forever be complete.
Walking to you, with the wind at my back,
Knowing with you, there's nothing I lack.
Come and get away, my love, my dove,
Let's soar high on the wings of love.
I loved her scarlet dress, a vision of delight,
In its embrace, everything felt right.
Take me away to where the forests whisper,
Where our love will never wither.
Walking to you, with each step I take,
Knowing with you, my heart will awake.
Come and get away, my dear, my light,
Let's dance beneath the stars tonight.
I loved her scarlet dress, a flame in the dark,
In its glow, I found my spark.
Take me away to where the dreams come true,
Where our love will forever renew.
Walking to you, with the stars as our guide,
In your arms, I'll forever reside.
Come and get away, my love, with haste,
Let's journey to a secret place.
I loved her scarlet dress, a symbol of grace,
In its folds, I found a sacred space.
Take me away to where the mountains rise,
Where our love will reach the skies.
Walking to you, with every breath I take,
Knowing with you, my heart won't break.
Come and get away, my dear, my light,
Let's chase away the shadows of the night.

I loved her scarlet dress, like a rose in bloom,
In its beauty, my heart found its room.
Take me away to where the rivers flow,
Where our love will continue to grow.
Walking to you, with the stars as our guide,
In your arms, I'll forever reside.
Come and get away, my love, with haste,
Let's journey to a secret place.
I loved her scarlet dress, a symbol of desire,
In its passion, I found a love to aspire.
Take me away to where the sunsets glow,
Where our love will forever flow.
Walking to you, with each beat of my heart,
Knowing with you, I'll never be apart.
Come and get away, my sweet, my flame,
Let's chase away the echoes of pain.
I loved her scarlet dress, a beacon in the night,
In its warmth, I found my guiding light.
Take me away to where the oceans meet,
Where our love will forever be complete.
Walking to you, with the wind at my back,
Knowing with you, there's nothing I lack.
Come and get away, my love, my dove,
Let's soar high on the wings of love.

Grace is lonely

His lover, a symphony of grace,
Each glance a melody, each touch a trace.
Through the mirror, he sees her smile,
A reflection of love that spans a mile.
Take me away now, to where passion ignites,
Where souls entwine under starry lights.
His heart beats fast at the thought of her,
A love so deep, so pure, so sure.
Through the mirror, their eyes meet,
And in that moment, their souls greet.
Take me away now, to where dreams come alive,
Where every touch makes us feel alive.
His lover's laughter, a sweet melody,
Filling his world with joy and glee.
Through the mirror, he sees her face,
A vision of beauty, a portrait of grace.
Take me away now, to where love blooms,
Where hearts dance amidst perfumed fumes.
His lover's touch, a gentle caress,
A soothing balm in times of distress.
Through the mirror, their love's reflection,
A bond unbroken, a divine connection.
Take me away now, to where passion flows,
Where the fire of love eternally glows.
His lover's voice, a melody divine,
Like sweet nectar, like aged wine.
Through the mirror, he sees her there,
A vision of beauty beyond compare.
Take me away now, to where dreams take flight,
Where love conquers all, in the darkest night.

His lover's scent, a fragrance rare,
Filling his senses, lingering in the air.
Through the mirror, their love's reflection,
A bond unbreakable, a divine connection.
Take me away now, to where love's embrace,
Where time stands still in a sacred space.
His lover's gaze, a beacon of light,
Guiding him through the darkest night.
Through the mirror, he sees her smile,
A love so pure, it spans every mile.
Take me away now, to where passion ignites,
Where hearts beat as one, through endless nights.
His lover's touch, a tender caress,
A whisper of love, a promise to bless.
Through the mirror, their eyes entwine,
In each other's gaze, they find the divine.
Take me away now, to where dreams come alive,
Where love's sweet melody forever thrives.
His lover's laughter, a joyful sound,
Filling his heart, his world around.
Through the mirror, he sees her face,
A vision of beauty, a portrait of grace.
Take me away now, to where love blooms,
Where hearts unite in sacred rooms.
His lover's touch, a gentle breeze,
Caressing his soul with effortless ease.
Through the mirror, their love's reflection,
A bond unbreakable, a divine connection.
Take me away now, to where passion flows,
Where love's sweet symphony forever grows.
His lover's voice, a song of love,
Echoing through the heavens above.

Through the mirror, he sees her there,
A vision of beauty beyond compare.
Take me away now, to where dreams take flight,
Where love conquers all, in the darkest night.
His lover's scent, a fragrant breeze,
Filling his senses, bringing him to ease.
Through the mirror, their love's reflection,
A bond unbreakable, a divine connection.
Take me away now, to where love's embrace,
Where time stands still in a sacred space.
His lover's gaze, a spark of fire,
Igniting his soul with passionate desire.
Through the mirror, he sees her smile,
A love so pure, it spans every mile.
Take me away now, to where passion ignites,
Where hearts beat as one, through endless nights.
His lover's touch, a tender caress,
A whisper of love, a promise to bless.
Through the mirror, their eyes entwine,
In each other's gaze, they find the divine.
Take me away now, to where dreams come alive,
Where love's sweet melody forever thrives.
His lover's laughter, a joyful sound,
Filling his heart, his world around.
Through the mirror, he sees her face,
A vision of beauty, a portrait of grace.
Take me away now, to where love blooms,
Where hearts unite in sacred rooms.
His lover's touch, a gentle breeze,
Caressing his soul with effortless ease.
Through the mirror, their love's reflection,
A bond unbreakable, a divine connection.

Take me away now, to where passion flows,
Where love's sweet symphony forever grows.
His lover's voice, a song of love,
Echoing through the heavens above.
Through the mirror, he sees her there,
A vision of beauty beyond compare.
Take me away now, to where dreams take flight,
Where love conquers all, in the darkest night.
His lover's scent, a fragrant breeze,
Filling his senses, bringing him to ease.
Through the mirror, their love's reflection,
A bond unbreakable, a divine connection.
Take me away now, to where love's embrace,
Where time stands still in a sacred space.
His lover's gaze, a spark of fire,
Igniting his soul with passionate desire.
Through the mirror, he sees her smile,
A love so pure, it spans every mile.
Take me away now, to where passion ignites,
Where hearts beat as one, through endless nights.
His lover's touch, a tender caress,
A whisper of love, a promise to bless.
Through the mirror, their eyes entwine,
In each other's gaze, they find the divine.
Take me away now, to where dreams come alive,
Where love's sweet melody forever thrives.
His lover's laughter, a joyful sound,
Filling his heart, his world around.
Through the mirror, he sees her face,
A vision of beauty, a portrait of grace.
Take me away now, to where love blooms,
Where hearts unite in sacred rooms.

His lover's touch, a gentle breeze,
Caressing his soul with effortless ease.
Through the mirror, their love's reflection,
A bond unbreakable, a divine connection.
Take me away now, to where passion flows,
Where love's sweet symphony forever grows.
His lover's voice, a song of love,
Echoing through the heavens above.
Through the mirror, he sees her there,
A vision of beauty beyond compare.
Take me away now, to where dreams take flight,
Where love conquers all, in the darkest night.
His lover's scent, a fragrant breeze,
Filling his senses, bringing him to ease.
Through the mirror, their love's reflection,
A bond unbreakable, a divine connection.
Take me away now, to where love's embrace,
Where time stands still in a sacred space.
His lover's gaze, a spark of fire,
Igniting his soul with passionate desire.
Through the mirror, he sees her smile,
A love so pure, it spans every mile.
Take me away now, to where passion ignites,
Where hearts beat as one, through endless nights.
His lover's touch, a tender caress,
A whisper of love, a promise to bless.
Through the mirror, their eyes entwine,
In each other's gaze, they find the divine.
Take me away now, to where dreams come alive,
Where love's sweet melody forever thrives.
His lover's laughter, a joyful sound,
Filling his heart, his world around.

Through the mirror, he sees her face,
A vision of beauty, a portrait of grace.
Take me away now, to where love blooms,
Where hearts unite in sacred rooms.
His lover's touch, a gentle breeze,
Caressing his soul with effortless ease.
Through the mirror, their love's reflection,
A bond unbreakable, a divine connection.
Take me away now, to where passion flows,
Where love's sweet symphony forever grows.
His lover's voice, a song of love,
Echoing through the heavens above.
Through the mirror, he sees her there,
A vision of beauty beyond compare.
Take me away now, to where dreams take flight,
Where love conquers all, in the darkest night.
His lover's scent, a fragrant breeze,
Filling his senses, bringing him to ease.
Through the mirror, their love's reflection,
A bond unbreakable, a divine connection.
Take me away now, to where love's embrace,
Where time stands still in a sacred space.
His lover's gaze, a spark of fire,
Igniting his soul with passionate desire.
Through the mirror, he sees her smile,
A love so pure, it spans every mile.
Take me away now, to where passion ignites,
Where hearts beat as one, through endless nights.
His lover's touch, a tender caress,
A whisper of love, a promise to bless.
Through the mirror, their eyes entwine,
In each other's gaze, they find the divine.

Take me away now, to where dreams come alive,
Where love's sweet melody forever thrives.
His lover's laughter, a joyful sound,
Filling his heart, his world around.
Through the mirror, he sees her face,
A vision of beauty, a portrait of grace.
Take me away now, to where love blooms,
Where hearts unite in sacred rooms.
His lover's touch, a gentle breeze,
Caressing his soul with effortless ease.
Through the mirror, their love's reflection,
A bond unbreakable, a divine connection.
Take me away now, to where passion flows,
Where love's sweet symphony forever grows.
His lover's voice, a song of love,
Echoing through the heavens above.
Through the mirror, he sees her there,
A vision of beauty beyond compare.
Take me away now, to where dreams take flight,
Where love conquers all, in the darkest night.
His lover's scent, a fragrant breeze,
Filling his senses, bringing him to ease.
Through the mirror, their love's reflection,
A bond unbreakable, a divine connection.
Take me away now, to where love's embrace,
Where time stands still in a sacred space.
His lover's gaze, a spark of fire,
Igniting his soul with passionate desire.
Through the mirror, he sees her smile,
A love so pure, it spans every mile.
Take me away now, to where passion ignites,
Where hearts beat as one, through endless nights.

His lover's touch, a tender caress,
A whisper of love, a promise to bless.
Through the mirror, their eyes entwine,
In each other's gaze, they find the divine.
Take me away now, to where dreams come alive,
Where love's sweet melody forever thrives.
His lover's laughter, a joyful sound,
Filling his heart, his world around.
Through the mirror, he sees her face,
A vision of beauty, a portrait of grace.
Take me away now, to where love blooms,
Where hearts unite in sacred rooms.
His lover's touch, a gentle breeze,
Caressing his soul with effortless ease.
Through the mirror, their love's reflection,
A bond unbreakable, a divine connection.
Take me away now, to where passion flows,
Where love's sweet symphony forever grows.
His lover's voice, a song of love,
Echoing through the heavens above.
Through the mirror, he sees her there,
A vision of beauty beyond compare.
Take me away now, to where dreams take flight,
Where love conquers all, in the darkest night.
His lover's scent, a fragrant breeze,
Filling his senses, bringing him to ease.
Through the mirror, their love's reflection,
A bond unbreakable, a divine connection.
Take me away now, to where love's embrace,
Where time stands still in a sacred space.
His lover's gaze, a spark of fire,
Igniting his soul with passionate desire.

Through the mirror, he sees her smile,
A love so pure, it spans every mile.
Take me away now, to where passion ignites,
Where hearts beat as one, through endless nights.
His lover's touch, a tender caress,
A whisper of love, a promise to bless.
Through the mirror, their eyes entwine,
In each other's gaze, they find the divine.
Take me away now, to where dreams come alive,
Where love's sweet melody forever thrives.
His lover's laughter, a joyful sound,
Filling his heart, his world around.
Through the mirror, he sees her face,
A vision of beauty, a portrait of grace.
Take me away now, to where love blooms,
Where hearts unite in sacred rooms.
His lover's touch, a gentle breeze,
Caressing his soul with effortless ease.
Through the mirror, their love's reflection,
A bond unbreakable, a divine connection.
Take me away now, to where passion flows,
Where love's sweet symphony forever grows.
His lover's voice, a song of love,
Echoing through the heavens above.
Through the mirror, he sees her there,
A vision of beauty beyond compare.
Take me away now, to where dreams take flight,
Where love conquers all, in the darkest night.
His lover's scent, a fragrant breeze,
Filling his senses, bringing him to ease.
Through the mirror, their love's reflection,
A bond unbreakable, a divine connection.

Take me away now, to where love's embrace,
Where time stands still in a sacred space.
His lover's gaze, a spark of fire,
Igniting his soul with passionate desire.
Through the mirror, he sees her smile,
A love so pure, it spans every mile.
Take me away now, to where passion ignites,
Where hearts beat as one, through endless nights.
His lover's touch, a tender caress,
A whisper of love, a promise to bless.
Through the mirror, their eyes entwine,
In each other's gaze, they find the divine.
Take me away now, to where dreams come alive,
Where love's sweet melody forever thrives.

Even he

In shadows deep, where darkness reigns,
The devil paces, consumed by pains.
His fiery eyes ablaze with desire,
Yearning for heaven's hallowed spire.
Back and forth, his steps resound,
Echoes of sin, his heart's rebound.
Yet amidst his tumultuous quest,
Lingers a flicker, a hopeful jest.
For even in the darkest night,
A glimmer of hope can take flight.
Perhaps beyond those pearly gates,
Redemption waits, forgiving fates.
With every stride, he dares to dream,
Of glimpsing grace in heaven's gleam.
To stand before the holy sight,
And find solace in the purest light.
Though demons whisper, doubts accrue,
He presses on, his spirit true.
For in the depths, where shadows dwell,
Hope blossoms forth, breaking his spell.
So let him pace, let him strive,
For even the devil may revive.
And in the end, may he find release,
Embraced by love, in eternal peace.

Silent stress

1. In silent steps, she danced with grace,
2. Amidst the whispers of divine embrace.
3. Each stride a hymn, each movement a prayer,
4. Her path illuminated, without a care.
5. Hand in hand with the divine,
6. She walked, transcending earthly line.
7. Through meadows blooming with faith's delight,
8. Her spirit soared, a radiant light.
9. With every step, a sacred vow,
10. Her heart ablaze, her soul aglow.
11. On pathways paved with mercy's touch,
12. She journeyed forth, her spirit lush.
13. In the stillness of the dawn's first light,
14. She walked with God, her beacon bright.
15. Through valleys deep and mountains high,
16. Her spirit soared, beyond the sky.
17. As she walked, the heavens sang,
18. Celestial chorus, with bells that rang.
19. With every stride, she found her place,
20. In the loving arms of divine grace.
21. Through storms of doubt and trials severe,
22. She pressed on, devoid of fear.
23. With faith as her guide, she marched on strong,
24. Her spirit echoing a heavenly song.
25. In the tenth circle, where saints reside,
26. She walked with God, side by side.
27. Surrounded by love, in eternal embrace,
28. Her journey complete, in heavenly grace.
29. In that sacred space, where angels sing,
30. She found her home, her soul taking wing.

31. Amongst the stars, her spirit soared,

32. Forever embraced by the divine Lord.

33. With each step, she left a trace,

34. Of faith and love, in every place.

35. Into the tenth circle, she gracefully trod,

36. A testament to her walk with God.

37. Through valleys of shadow, she persevered,

38. Guided by faith, her spirit cleared.

39. With each step, she drew near,

40. To the tenth circle, without fear.

41. Hand in hand, they walked as one,

42. Underneath the eternal sun.

43. In the presence of divine light,

44. She found her home, shining bright.

45. Through trials and tribulations, she held on tight,

46. Trusting in God's guiding light.

47. With each step, a journey begun,

48. Towards the tenth circle, where she would become.

49. In the tenth circle, she found her place,

50. Wrapped in the warmth of divine embrace.

51. With every step, she drew near,

52. To the heart of God, without fear.

53. Through the valleys of despair and woe,

54. She walked with God, her spirit aglow.

55. In the tenth circle, where love abides,

56. She found her home, by His side.

57. With every step, she left behind,

58. A trail of faith, pure and kind.

59. Into the tenth circle, she gracefully strode,

60. In the presence of her heavenly abode.

61. Through trials and tribulations, she stayed true,

62. Walking with God, her spirit renewed.

63. In the tenth circle, where angels sing,
64. She found her home, under heavenly wing.
65. With each step, she drew near,
66. To the tenth circle, without fear.
67. Guided by faith, her spirit soared,
68. Into the arms of her divine Lord.
69. Through storms and tempests, she held on tight,
70. Trusting in God's guiding light.
71. In the tenth circle, where saints reside,
72. She found her home, her spirit untied.
73. In the presence of divine grace,
74. She walked with God, in sacred space.
75. Through trials and tribulations, she stayed strong,
76. Until she reached where she belonged.
77. Into the tenth circle, she made her way,
78. Guided by faith, come what may.
79. In the loving embrace of her divine King,
80. She found her home, where angels sing.

Lover lost

In the garden of memories, you linger still,
Your laughter echoing, a bittersweet thrill.
In every whispered breeze, I hear your name,
A lover lost, yet hearts still aflame.
Your absence a void, a silent ache,
A love once vibrant, now a heartbreak.
In dreams, you dance, just out of reach,
A phantom of love, I yearn to beseech.
Your smile, a beacon in the darkest night,
A memory etched, burning bright.
In every tear shed, a love confessed,
A heart once whole, now distressed.
In the tapestry of time, our story weaves,
A tale of love, with shattered beliefs.
In every echo of laughter, I find your trace,
A lover lost, in this endless chase.
Your touch, a memory etched in skin,
A gentle caress, lost in sin.
In every whispered prayer, I seek your grace,
A lover lost, in this empty space.
In the silence of solitude, your voice I hear,
A lover's lament, drawing near.
In every heartbeat, I feel your touch,
A love once cherished, now too much.
Your gaze, a promise in the starlit sky,
A fleeting moment, passing by.
In every sunrise, I see your face,
A lover lost, in this empty place.
In the symphony of sorrow, your song remains,
A haunting melody, coursing through veins.

In every breath taken, I taste your kiss,
A lover lost, in this abyss.
Your love, a flame that once burned bright,
A flickering ember, lost in the night.
In every whisper of wind, I hear your plea,
A lover lost, now set free.
In the gallery of my heart, you're framed in gold,
A masterpiece of love, forever bold.
In every heartbeat, I feel your presence near,
A lover lost, but still so dear.
Your essence, a fragrance in the air,
A memory cherished, beyond compare.
In every moment, I feel your touch,
A lover lost, I miss you much.
In the pages of time, our love unfolds,
A story of passion, yet untold.
In every sunrise, I seek your gaze,
A lover lost, in these endless days.
Your laughter, a melody in the night,
A symphony of joy, burning bright.
In every heartbeat, I feel your embrace,
A lover lost, in this sacred space.
In the tapestry of fate, our threads entwine,
A love eternal, a bond divine.
In every whisper of love, I hear your plea,
A lover lost, come back to me.

I'm the beauty

In the quiet of night, her heart found peace,
In the warmth of my embrace, troubles ceased.
In the depths of her soul, she found solace with me,
In the sanctuary of love, she felt truly free.
In the chaos of life, she found calm,
In the shelter of my love, like a healing balm.
In the symphony of our love, she found her song,
In the harmony of our hearts, where she belonged.
In the embrace of our love, she found her home,
In the depths of our bond, she was never alone.
In the laughter we shared, she found delight,
In the moments together, everything felt right.
In the silence of our togetherness, she found meaning,
In the depths of our connection, her heart was gleaming.
In the dance of our souls, she found rhythm,
In the melody of our love, she found her hymn.
In the warmth of our touch, she felt alive,
In the tenderness of our love, she learned to thrive.
In the light of our love, she found her way,
In the darkness of despair, she knew I'd stay.
In the depths of her love for me, she found her strength,
In the belief in our love, she went to great lengths.
In the dreams we shared, she found her wings,
In the reality of our love, she felt like a queen.
In the gentleness of my words, she found peace,
In the passion of our love, her worries ceased.
In the bond we shared, she found her anchor,
In the depths of our love, she found her banker.
In the journey of love, she found her guide,
In the depths of my love, she felt dignified.

In the embrace of our love, she found her light,
In the shadows of doubt, she held on tight.
In the adventure of our love, she found her thrill,
In the moments we shared, time stood still.
In the whispers of our hearts, she found her truth,
In the depths of our love, she found her youth.
In the magic of our love, she found her spark,
In the depths of our connection, she left her mark.
In the eternity of our love, she found her forever,
In the depths of her heart, she knew we'd never sever.
In the symphony of our love, she found her voice,
In the depths of our connection, she made her choice.
In the beauty of our love, she found her art,
In the depths of her soul, she felt my heart.
In the whispers of our love, she found her song,
In the depths of our bond, she felt strong.
In the depths of our love, she found her peace,
In the chaos of life, her worries would cease.
In the depths of our love, she found her shore,
In the vastness of the ocean, she wanted more.
In the embrace of our love, she found her home,
In the depths of our connection, she'd never roam.
In the laughter we shared, she found her joy,
In the depths of our love, she felt like a buoy.
In the gentle caress of my touch, she found her calm,
In the depths of our love, she found her psalm.
In the beauty of our love, she found her grace,
In the depths of her heart, she found her place.
In the whispers of our love, she found her peace,
In the depths of our connection, worries would cease.
In the dance of our souls, she found her rhythm,
In the melody of our love, she found her hymn.

In the depths of our love, she found her ground,
In the world spinning without me, she found no sound.
In the echoes of our laughter, she found her cheer,
In the emptiness without me, she found fear.
In the vastness of the universe, she found her place,
In the world spinning without me, she found no grace.
In the depths of her love for me, she found her might,
In the absence of my presence, she found no light.
In the whispers of our love, she found her tune,
In the world spinning without me, she felt marooned.
In the symphony of our hearts, she found her beat,
In the silence without me, she felt incomplete.
In the whispers of our love, she found her peace,
In the world spinning without me, worries would increase.
In the embrace of our love, she found her sanctuary,
In the world spinning without me, she felt solitary.
In the laughter we shared, she found her joy,
In the absence of my presence, life felt like a ploy.
In the echoes of our love, she found her song,
In the world spinning without me, she felt wronged.
In the depths of our love, she found her truth,
In the world spinning without me, she felt uncouth.
In the dance of our souls, she found her grace,
In the absence of my presence, she felt out of place.
In the whispers of our love, she found her home,
In the world spinning without me, she felt alone.
In the depths of her love for me, she found her way,
In the absence of my presence, she felt astray.
In the symphony of our love, she found her tune,
In the world spinning without me, she felt marooned.
In the embrace of our love, she found her light,
In the absence of my presence, she felt like a kite.

In the laughter we shared, she found her glee,
In the world spinning without me, she felt free.
In the echoes of our love, she found her voice,
In the absence of my presence, she felt no choice.
In the depths of our love, she found her shore,
In the vastness of the ocean, she wanted more.
In the whispers of our love, she found her calm,
In the absence of my presence, she felt qualm.

In the ending

In the embrace of our love, she found her serenity,
In the depths of my soul, she found tranquility.
In the whispers of our hearts, she found her peace,
In the presence of my love, her worries would cease.
In the warmth of our connection, she felt secure,
In the stillness of our moments, her doubts would blur.
In the shelter of my arms, she found her rest,
In the comfort of my love, she felt blessed.
In the depth of our bond, she found her solace,
In the embrace of my love, she found grace.
In the rhythm of our love, she found her calm,
In the sanctuary of my presence, she felt no harm.
In the silence of our togetherness, she found her ease,
In the communion of our souls, her fears would ease.
In the depths of our love, she found her refuge,
In the essence of my being, she found her deluge.
In the stillness of the night, she felt embraced,
In the whisper of my love, she found her place.
In the gaze of my eyes, she found her shelter,
In the warmth of my touch, she felt lighter.
In the depths of my heart, she found her home,
In the love we shared, she'd never roam.
In the rhythm of our breath, she found her peace,
In the embrace of my arms, her worries would cease.
In the sanctuary of my presence, she felt secure,
In the depths of my love, she found her allure.
In the silence of our connection, she found her voice,
In the strength of our bond, she made her choice.
In the gentleness of my touch, she found her calm,
In the depths of my love, she felt no qualm.

In the safety of my embrace, she found her solace,
In the depths of my love, she found her palace.
In the stillness of our moments, she felt serene,
In the depths of my love, she felt unseen.
In the whispers of our hearts, she found her melody,
In the embrace of my love, she felt free.
In the depths of my soul, she found her serenity,
In the presence of my love, she felt eternity.
In the warmth of my embrace, she found her rest,
In the depths of my love, she felt truly blessed.
In the shelter of my arms, she found her peace,
In the depth of our connection, her fears would cease.
In the embrace of my love, she found her ease,
In the depths of my heart, she found her release.
In the sanctuary of my presence, she felt serene,
In the whispers of my love, she felt unseen.
In the warmth of my touch, she found her calm,
In the depths of my love, she felt no qualm.
In the depths of my heart, she found her solace,
In the embrace of my love, she felt whole.
In the rhythm of our love, she found her song,
In the depths of my soul, she felt strong.
In the shelter of my embrace, she felt secure,
In the presence of my love, she felt sure.
In the depths of my love, she found her peace,
In the sanctuary of my presence, her worries would cease.
In the stillness of our moments, she felt embraced,
In the whispers of my love, she felt encased.

Move your hips

In the sway of her hips, a mesmerizing dance,
Captivating all with just a glance.
With each step, she weaved a tale,
In the rhythm of life, she set sail.
Her laughter, a melody, pure and bright,
Guiding hearts through the darkest night.
With grace she moved, like a flowing stream,
A sight to behold, a beautiful dream.
In the sparkle of her eyes, mischief and glee,
A whirlwind of charm, for all to see.
Her confidence radiated, bold and true,
In her presence, the world felt anew.
In every gesture, a story told,
A tapestry of elegance, manifold.
With every sway, she stole the show,
A force of nature, with a radiant glow.
In the way she moved, a symphony of grace,
Leaving trails of awe in her trace.
With each twirl and spin, she cast a spell,
Enchanting hearts, oh, how well!
In the rhythm of her stride, a dance divine,
A vision of beauty, so fine.
In her movement, a magic unfurled,
An enchantress, captivating the world.
With each flick of her hair, a spell was cast,
In her presence, time flew by fast.
In the way she moved, oh, what a sight,
A vision of loveliness, pure delight.
In the sway of her hips, the world stood still,
Captivated by her every thrill.

With every step, she owned the floor,
A goddess of movement, forevermore.
In the way she moved, she stole the show,
A sight to behold, aglow.
With every gesture, she left a mark,
In the hearts of all, a spark.
In the rhythm of her dance, she found her groove,
A testament to her spirit, so smooth.
In the way she moved, she lit up the night,
A beacon of joy, burning bright.
With each movement, she captured hearts,
In her grace, she played her part.
In the sway of her hips, a symphony played,
In her dance, a legacy made.
With every twirl and turn, she left her mark,
In the way she moved, she left a spark.
In the grace of her steps, she found her voice,
In the rhythm of life, she made her choice.
With every sway, she stole the scene,
In her movement, a beauty unseen.
In the way she moved, she painted the sky,
A masterpiece of grace, soaring high.
With each step, she danced with flair,
A vision of elegance, beyond compare.
In the rhythm of her dance, she found her place,
A dance of life, full of grace.
In the way she moved, she conquered all,
A queen of dance, standing tall.
With every twirl and spin, she lit up the room,
In her movement, a sense of bloom.
In the grace of her steps, she found her stride,
In the dance of life, she found her guide.

With every gesture, she told a story,
In her movement, a glimpse of glory.
In the sway of her hips, a world unfurled,
In the way she moved, she ruled the world.

Cyclone

In the silence of departure, echoes resound,
Leaving me alone, on uncertain ground.
In the wake of your absence, shadows grow,
Leaving me alone, in the undertow.
With every step you take, a piece of me,
Left alone, to navigate the sea.
In the void you leave behind, I wander lost,
Left alone, to count the cost.
In the space you once filled, emptiness reigns,
Left alone, to bear the strains.
With your goodbye, the world feels hollow,
Left alone, to drown in sorrow.
In the echo of your voice, I find no solace,
Left alone, in this empty palace.
With your departure, the sky turns grey,
Left alone, to face the day.
In the stillness of your absence, I ache,
Left alone, my heart to break.
With every memory, a pang of pain,
Left alone, in this endless rain.
In the silence of goodbye, I mourn,
Left alone, to weather the storm.
With your leaving, the stars lose their shine,
Left alone, in this heart of mine.
In the echoes of your footsteps, I'm left behind,
Left alone, with memories entwined.
With every tear shed, a piece of me gone,
Left alone, to carry on.
In the void you leave, I search in vain,
Left alone, to bear the strain.

With your departure, the world grows cold,
Left alone, as the story's told.
In the quiet of the night, I hear your sigh,
Left alone, beneath the sky.
With your leaving, the colors fade,
Left alone, in this masquerade.
In the wake of your absence, I find no peace,
Left alone, my heart to cease.
With every thought of you, a silent plea,
Left alone, in this reverie.
In the silence of goodbye, I stand alone,
Left alone, in this twilight zone.
With your departure, I'm adrift at sea,
Left alone, with only me.
In the echoes of your laughter, I find no joy,
Left alone, my heart to deploy.
With every whispered farewell, a tear I shed,
Left alone, in this empty bed.
In the hollow of your goodbye, I am bereft,
Left alone, with nothing left.
With your leaving, the world seems still,
Left alone, against my will.
In the aftermath of your departure, I remain,
Left alone, to bear the pain.
With every passing moment, I feel the weight,
Left alone, to meet my fate.
In the wake of your absence, I stand alone,
Left alone, with heart of stone.
With your goodbye, the world fades away,
Left alone, in the disarray.
In the silence of your departure, I am undone,
Left alone, to face the sun.

With every memory, a ghost of you,
Left alone, what am I to do?
In the shadow of your leaving, I am left to grieve,
Left alone, with naught to achieve.
With your departure, the world feels small,
Left alone, to recall.
In the silence of goodbye, I am alone,
Left alone, to make it on my own.
With your leaving, the world turns grey,
Left alone, to find my way.
In the absence of your presence, I am left alone,
Left alone, to atone.
With your departure, the world spins on,
Left alone, to carry on.
In the aftermath of your goodbye, I remain,
Left alone, in this refrain.
With every step you take, I am left behind,
Left alone, to seek what I cannot find.
In the silence of your leaving, I am adrift,
Left alone, to sift.
With your departure, the world feels cold,
Left alone, to grow old.
In the echo of your farewell, I am left alone,
Left alone, in this cyclone.
With every thought of you, I am alone,
Left alone, to atone.
In the wake of your absence, I am left to cope,
Left alone, with fading hope.
With your goodbye, the world feels strange,
Left alone, in this change.
In the void you leave behind, I am left alone,
Left alone, to find my own.

With your departure, I am left alone,
Left alone, to mourn.
In the silence of your goodbye, I am left to mourn,
Left alone, in this forlorn.
With every memory, I am left alone,
Left alone, in this cyclone.
In the shadow of your leaving, I am left alone,
Left alone, to atone.
With your departure, I am left alone,
Left alone, to face the unknown.
In the silence of your absence, I am left alone,
Left alone, to make it on my own.
With your goodbye, I am left alone,
Left alone, in this cyclone.
In the wake of your leaving, I am left alone,
Left alone, to find my own.
With every thought of you, I am left alone,
Left alone, in this cyclone.
In the void you leave behind, I am left alone,
Left alone, to atone.
With your departure, I am left alone,
Left alone, to mourn.
In the silence of your goodbye, I am left to mourn,
Left alone, in this forlorn.
With every memory, I am left alone,
Left alone, in this cyclone.
In the shadow of your leaving, I am left alone,
Left alone, to atone.
With your departure, I am left alone,
Left alone, to face the unknown.
In the silence of your absence, I am left alone,
Left alone, to make it on my own.

With your goodbye, I am left alone,
Left alone, in this cyclone.
In the wake of your leaving, I am left alone,
Left alone, to find my own.
With every thought of you, I am left alone,
Left alone, in this cyclone.
In the void you leave behind, I am left alone,
Left alone, to atone.
With your departure, I am left alone,
Left alone, to mourn.
In the silence of your goodbye, I am left to mourn,
Left alone, in this forlorn.
With every memory, I am left alone,
Left alone, in this cyclone.
In the shadow of your leaving, I am left alone,
Left alone, to atone.
With your departure, I am left alone,
Left alone, to face the unknown.
In the silence of your absence, I am left alone,
Left alone, to make it on my own.
With your goodbye, I am left alone,
Left alone, in this cyclone.
In the wake of your leaving, I am left alone,
Left alone, to find my own.
With every thought of you, I am left alone,
Left alone, in this cyclone.
In the void you leave behind, I am left alone,
Left alone, to atone.
With your departure, I am left alone,
Left alone, to mourn.
In the silence of your goodbye, I am left to mourn,
Left alone, in this forlorn.

With every memory, I am left alone,
Left alone, in this cyclone.
In the shadow of your leaving, I am left alone,
Left alone, to atone.
With your departure, I am left alone,
Left alone, to face the unknown.
In the silence of your absence, I am left alone,
Left alone, to make
it on my own.
With your goodbye, I am left alone,
Left alone, in this cyclone.
In the wake of your leaving, I am left alone,
Left alone, to find my own.
With every thought of you, I am left alone,
Left alone, in this cyclone.
In the void you leave behind, I am left alone,
Left alone, to atone.
With your departure, I am left alone,
Left alone, to mourn.
In the silence of your goodbye, I am left to mourn,
Left alone, in this forlorn.
With every memory, I am left alone,
Left alone, in this cyclone.
In the shadow of your leaving, I am left alone,
Left alone, to atone.
With your departure, I am left alone,
Left alone, to face the unknown.
In the silence of your absence, I am left alone,
Left alone, to make it on my own.
With your goodbye, I am left alone,
Left alone, in this cyclone.
In the wake of your leaving, I am left alone,

Left alone, to find my own.
With every thought of you, I am left alone,
Left alone, in this cyclone.
In the void you leave behind, I am left alone,
Left alone, to atone.
With your departure, I am left alone,
Left alone, to mourn.
In the silence of your goodbye, I am left to mourn,
Left alone, in this forlorn.
With every memory, I am left alone,
Left alone, in this cyclone.
In the shadow of your leaving, I am left alone,
Left alone, to atone.
With your departure, I am left alone,
Left alone, to face the unknown.
In the silence of your absence, I am left alone,
Left alone, to make it on my own.
With your goodbye, I am left alone,
Left alone, in this cyclone.
In the wake of your leaving, I am left alone,
Left alone, to find my own.
With every thought of you, I am left alone,
Left alone, in this cyclone.
In the void you leave behind, I am left alone,
Left alone, to atone.
With your departure, I am left alone,
Left alone, to mourn.
In the silence of your goodbye, I am left to mourn,
Left alone, in this forlorn.
With every memory, I am left alone,
Left alone, in this cyclone.
In the shadow of your leaving, I am left alone,

Left alone, to atone.
With your departure, I am left alone,
Left alone, to face the unknown.
In the silence of your absence, I am left alone,
Left alone, to make it on my own.
With your goodbye, I am left alone,
Left alone, in this cyclone.
In the wake of your leaving, I am left alone,
Left alone, to find my own.
With every thought of you, I am left alone,
Left alone, in this cyclone.
In the void you leave behind, I am left alone,
Left alone, to atone.
With your departure, I am left alone,
Left alone, to mourn.
In the silence of your goodbye, I am left to mourn,
Left alone, in this forlorn.
With every memory, I am left alone,
Left alone, in this cyclone.
In the shadow of your leaving, I am left alone,
Left alone, to atone.
With your departure, I am left alone,
Left alone, to face the unknown.
In the silence of your absence, I am left alone,
Left alone, to make it on my own.
With your goodbye, I am left alone,
Left alone, in this cyclone.
In the wake of your leaving, I am left alone,
Left alone, to find my own.
With every thought of you, I am left alone,
Left alone, in this cyclone.
In the void you leave behind, I am left alone,

Left alone, to atone.
With your departure, I am left alone,
Left alone, to mourn.
In the silence of your goodbye, I am left to mourn,
Left alone, in this forlorn.
With every memory, I am left alone,
Left alone, in this cyclone.

Flying high

In the realm of my heart, they once shone bright,
Girls, girls who vanished from sight.
Their laughter echoed in the corridors of my mind,
Girls, girls who left me behind.
With every step they took, a piece of me went too,
Girls, girls who bid adieu.
In the echoes of their absence, I found no reprieve,
Girls, girls who chose to leave.
Their absence a void, a silent plea,
Girls, girls who set me free.
With their departure, the world felt cold,
Girls, girls who left me to unfold.
In the wake of their leaving, I stood alone,
Girls, girls who carved their own.
Their memories lingered, haunting my dreams,
Girls, girls who tore at the seams.
With every thought of them, a pang of pain,
Girls, girls who left a stain.
In the silence of their absence, I searched in vain,
Girls, girls who caused this strain.
Their laughter, a melody I longed to hear,
Girls, girls who disappeared.
With their goodbye, the world lost its hue,
Girls, girls who bid adieu.
In the whispers of their departure, I found despair,
Girls, girls who left me in the air.
Their absence a weight I couldn't bear,
Girls, girls who vanished into thin air.
With every memory, a tear I shed,
Girls, girls who left me in dread.

In the void they left, I stumbled alone,
Girls, girls who turned to stone.
Their presence, once a comfort, now a void,
Girls, girls who left me destroyed.
With their leaving, my heart grew cold,
Girls, girls who left me untold.
In the aftermath of their departure, I stood bereft,
Girls, girls who left me adrift.
Their absence a wound that refused to heal,
Girls, girls who left me to feel.
With every whisper of their name, a silent plea,
Girls, girls who left me to be.
In the silence of their absence, I found no solace,
Girls, girls who left without malice.
Their laughter, a memory etched in time,
Girls, girls who left me to climb.
With their goodbye, the world lost its shine,
Girls, girls who left me to pine.
In the shadows of their leaving, I found no reprieve,
Girls, girls who made me grieve.
Their absence a presence that lingered on,
Girls, girls who left me alone.
With every thought of them, a void grew wide,
Girls, girls who left me to bide.
In the silence of their departure, I found no peace,
Girls, girls who made my heart cease.
Their laughter, once music to my ears,
Girls, girls who left me in tears.
With their leaving, the world lost its grace,
Girls, girls who left without a trace.
In the echoes of their absence, I found no light,
Girls, girls who took flight.

Their absence a void, a gaping hole,
Girls, girls who took their toll.
With every memory, I felt the ache,
Girls, girls who left me to forsake.
In the wake of their leaving, I found no reprieve,
Girls, girls who made me grieve.
Their laughter, a melody lost in time,
Girls, girls who left me to climb.
With their goodbye, the world grew dim,
Girls, girls who left me to swim.
In the shadows of their departure, I found no solace,
Girls, girls who left me to face.
Their absence a weight I couldn't bear,
Girls, girls who left me to despair.
With every thought of them, a tear I shed,
Girls, girls who left me to dread.
In the silence of their absence, I searched in vain,
Girls, girls who left me in pain.
Their laughter, a memory I hold dear,
Girls, girls who disappeared.
With their leaving, my world fell apart,
Girls, girls who broke my heart.
In the echoes of their absence, I found no peace,
Girls, girls who made my heart cease.
Their absence a void, a silent scream,
Girls, girls who left me in a dream.
With every memory, a piece of me went too,
Girls, girls who bid adieu.
In the wake of their leaving, I stood alone,
Girls, girls who carved their own.
Their memories lingered, haunting my soul,
Girls, girls who took their toll.

With their departure, the world lost its shine,
Girls, girls who left me behind.
In the whispers of their absence, I found no solace,
Girls, girls who left without malice.
Their laughter, once a comfort, now a pain,
Girls, girls who left me in vain.
With their goodbye, the world lost its grace,
Girls, girls who left without a trace.
In the shadows of their leaving, I found no reprieve,
Girls, girls who made me grieve.
Their absence a presence that lingered on,
Girls, girls who left me alone.
With every thought of them, a void grew wide,
Girls, girls who left me to bide.
In the silence of their departure, I found no peace,
Girls, girls who made my heart cease.
Their laughter, once music to my ears,
Girls, girls who left me in tears.
With their leaving, the world lost its hue,
Girls, girls who left me to pine.
In the echoes of their absence, I found no light,
Girls, girls who took flight.

New world

In her own world, she dances with stars,
    Inviting me to journey, to break through bars.
In her universe, colors blend and swirl,
    A kaleidoscope of wonders, an enchanting pearl.
In her sanctuary, whispers of dreams take flight,
    Where reality and fantasy intertwine in the night.
In her realm, time bends and slows,
    A canvas of moments, where anything goes.
In her domain, melodies echo and soar,
    Guiding me to her world, to explore.
In her kingdom, laughter echoes loud,
    A symphony of joy, lifting every cloud.
In her sanctuary, peace reigns supreme,
    A haven of tranquility, like a dream.
In her cosmos, love knows no bounds,
    Where hearts connect, in harmonic sounds.
In her paradise, beauty blooms anew,
    Inviting me to see, to feel, to pursue.
In her realm, sorrows gently fade,
    As she beckons me to her serenade.
In her universe, mysteries unfold,
    A tapestry of secrets waiting to be told.
In her sanctuary, fears dissipate,
    As she welcomes me to her gate.
In her domain, fantasies take flight,
    A wonderland of magic, pure delight.
In her kingdom, kindness reigns supreme,
    As she shows me her world, like a dream.
In her cosmos, dreams take shape,
    Inviting me to dance, to escape.

In her paradise, serenity flows,
As she invites me to wander, to decompose.
In her realm, hopes take flight,
As she shows me her world, full of light.
In her universe, dreams come alive,
A realm of possibility, where we thrive.
In her sanctuary, love's embrace,
As she shows me her world, with grace.
In her domain, time stands still,
As she invites me to her will.
In her kingdom, joy abounds,
As she shows me her world, profound.
In her cosmos, dreams take flight,
As she invites me to her sight.
In her paradise, love blooms anew,
As she shows me her world, so true.
In her realm, beauty shines bright,
As she invites me to her light.
In her universe, laughter fills the air,
As she shows me her world, beyond compare.
In her sanctuary, peace reigns supreme,
As she shows me her world, like a dream.
In her domain, love knows no bounds,
As she shows me her world, profound.
In her kingdom, dreams come true,
As she shows me her world, anew.
In her cosmos, beauty lies within,
As she shows me her world, to begin.
In her paradise, wonders unfold,
As she shows me her world, bold.
In her realm, love's melody plays,
As she shows me her world, in a daze.

In her universe, magic takes flight,
As she shows me her world, with delight.
In her sanctuary, dreams find their way,
As she shows me her world, to stay.
In her domain, possibilities bloom,
As she shows me her world, in full bloom.
In her kingdom, love's embrace,
As she shows me her world, with grace.
In her cosmos, stars alight,
As she shows me her world, so bright.
In her paradise, dreams come true,
As she shows me her world, anew.
In her realm, beauty unfurls,
As she shows me her world, in swirls.
In her universe, dreams take flight,
As she shows me her world, so right.
In her sanctuary, love prevails,
As she shows me her world, without fails.
In her domain, peace resides,
As she shows me her world, with strides.
In her kingdom, joy abounds,
As she shows me her world, with sounds.

Dancing in the pale moonlight

In the fleeting dance of time, I found my solace in her embrace.
Each moment with her was a symphony of love.
Her laughter echoed through the corridors of my heart.
Time stood still when I held her close.
In her eyes, I found a universe of love.
Like autumn leaves, our love painted the passage of time.
Her touch lingered like a sweet melody.
In the tapestry of time, she was the brightest thread.
With her, every moment felt like an eternity.
In the whispers of the wind, I heard her name.
Her smile was the sun that brightened my days.
With her by my side, I was never afraid of time's passage.
In the twilight of memories, she remains my brightest star.
Our love was a timeless tale written in the sands of time.
With her, even the mundane became magical.
In the silence of the night, her presence was my comfort.
Her love was a beacon guiding me through life's storms.
Like a gentle breeze, her love swept through my soul.
In her embrace, I found sanctuary from the chaos of time.
She was the melody that played in the background of my life.
With her, every moment was a cherished memory.
Her laughter was the soundtrack of our love story.
In the gallery of my mind, her image remains etched in time.
With her, I discovered the beauty of living in the moment.
Her love was the compass that guided me home.
In the ebb and flow of time, she was my constant.
With her, I learned to savor the sweetness of now.
Her presence was the sunrise of my every day.
In the depths of her eyes, I found my forever.
With her, even the darkest nights were filled with stars.

Her love was the melody that played in my heart's chambers.
In the mosaic of memories, she was the centerpieces.
With her, I learned that love transcends time and space.
Her laughter was the echo that resonated in my soul.
In the book of my life, she was the most beautiful chapter.
With her, every moment felt like a lifetime.
Her love was the anchor that kept me grounded in the present.
In the rhythm of her heartbeat, I found my home.
With her, I experienced the magic of every passing second.
Her touch was the brushstroke that painted my world.
In the dance of time, she was my favorite partner.
With her, I learned that time is best spent in love.
Her love was the melody that played on repeat in my heart.
In the tapestry of our love, every thread was woven with care.
With her, I found meaning in the passage of time.
Her laughter was the soundtrack of our shared moments.
In the quiet moments, her presence whispered love.
With her, I learned to appreciate the beauty of each moment.
Her love was the poetry that danced on my lips.
In the symphony of life, she was my favorite note.
With her, I discovered the magic of being present.
Her touch was the warmth that filled my soul.
In the melody of our love, I found my rhythm.
With her, time was but a fleeting concept.
Her love was the melody that played on the strings of my heart.
In the canvas of time, she was my masterpiece.
With her, I learned that love knows no bounds.
Her laughter was the melody that echoed in my dreams.
In the whispers of the night, her voice was my lullaby.
With her, I learned that every moment is a gift.
Her love was the compass that guided me through life's maze.
In the silence of the dawn, her presence was my serenity.

With her, I discovered the beauty of the here and now.
Her touch was the gentle caress that soothed my soul.
In the tapestry of our memories, she was the brightest thread.
With her, time was but a fleeting whisper in the wind.
Her love was the melody that played in the depths of my soul.
In the dance of life, she was my perfect partner.
With her, I learned that love is the only true measure of time.
Her laughter was the music that filled my days with joy.
In the poetry of our love, every word was a testament to our bond.
With her, I discovered the beauty of the present moment.
Her love was the light that guided me through the darkest nights.
In the tapestry of time, she was my favorite chapter.
With her, every moment felt like eternity in a single heartbeat.
Her touch was the warmth that ignited my soul.
In the symphony of our love, every note was harmonious.
With her, I learned that time is best spent in love's embrace.
Her laughter was the melody that danced in the air.
In the silence of the night, her presence was my solace.
With her, I discovered the beauty of living in the moment.
Her love was the compass that guided me through life's storms.
In the whispers of the wind, I heard her name.
With her, every moment was a cherished memory.
Her touch was the gentle caress that soothed my soul.
In the tapestry of our love, every thread was woven with care.
With her, I learned that love knows no bounds.
Her laughter was the music that filled my days with joy.
In the poetry of our love, every word was a testament to our bond.
With her, I found meaning in the passage of time.
Her love was the melody that played on the strings of my heart.
In the dance of life, she was my perfect partner.
With her, I discovered the beauty of the present moment.
Her touch was the warmth that ignited my soul.

In the symphony of our love, every note was harmonious.
With her, every moment felt like eternity in a single heartbeat.
Her laughter was the melody that danced in the air.
In the silence of the night, her presence was my solace.
With her, I learned that time is best spent in love's embrace.
Her love was the compass that guided me through life's storms.

www.ingramcontent.com/pod-product-compliance
Lightning Source LLC
Chambersburg PA
CBHW050806250726
48653CB00006B/2107